| catalogue 20 |

LES ENLUMINURES

FOUR REMARKABLE MANUSCRIPTS FROM THE MIDDLE AGES

Christopher de Hamel
Preface Sandra Hindman

EXHIBITION

LES ENLUMINURES New York
October 17-23, 2018

TEFAF New York Fall
October 27-31, 2018

FINE ARTS Paris
November 7-11, 2018

Les Enluminures ltd.

23 EAST 73RD STREET
7TH FLOOR, PENTHOUSE
NEW YORK, NY 10021
TEL: (212) 717 7273
NEWYORK@LESENLUMINURES.COM

Les Enluminures ltd.

ONE MAGNIFICENT MILE
980 NORTH MICHIGAN AVE.
SUITE 1330
CHICAGO, IL 60611
TEL: (773) 929 5986
CHICAGO@LESENLUMINURES.COM

Les Enluminures

1, RUE JEAN-JACQUES ROUSSEAU
75001 PARIS
TEL: (33) 01 42 60 15 58
INFO@LESENLUMINURES.COM

ISBN 978-0-9971842-7-3

FULL DESCRIPTIONS AVAILABLE ON
WWW.LESENLUMINURES.COM

| catalogue 20 |

LES ENLUMINURES

FOUR REMARKABLE MANUSCRIPTS FROM THE MIDDLE AGES

Christopher de Hamel
Preface Sandra Hindman

PAUL HOLBERTON PUBLISHING, 89 BOROUGH HIGH STREET, LONDON SE1 1NL
WWW.PAUL-HOLBERTON.NET
FOR LES ENLUMINURES • PARIS • CHICAGO • NEW YORK

CONTENTS

PREFACE

This is a catalogue of recent acquisitions by Les Enluminures of "remarkable manuscripts." We have borrowed the title from Christopher de Hamel's award-winning book *Meetings with Remarkable Manuscripts* (Penguin 2016), in which he travels to libraries throughout the world to share with us his experience looking at extraordinary manuscripts. Like the manuscripts in de Hamel's book, these four richly illuminated examples bring us in contact with wondrous objects surviving from the medieval world. Unlike the manuscripts in de Hamel's book, however, these manuscripts are not housed in libraries and museums. They are for sale.

It is remarkable that in the twenty-first century such examples remain on the open market. They have not been in public view for the better part of a century, and in one case for more than four centuries. Each manuscript transports us back to daily life in the Middle Ages. In all but one instance, we may even know the original owner of the manuscript, and we can quite literally imagine ourselves peering over his or her shoulder as we gaze at its pages.

Behind every book there is a team of individuals who worked hard to bring it to completion. I would like to thank my colleagues at Les Enluminures, who helped in countless ways: among them, Gaia Grizzi, Laura Light, and Keegan Goepfert. Thanks also to Matthew Westerby, our consummate copy-editor.

Come discover the stories behind these remarkable manuscripts made so vivid in the following pages by the incomparable Christopher de Hamel.

SANDRA HINDMAN
PRESIDENT AND FOUNDER, LES ENLUMINURES

INTRODUCTION

I wrote a book a couple of years ago called *Meetings with Remarkable Manuscripts*. It was an attempt to convey the thrill and fascination of visiting libraries and museums worldwide and of examining the originals of well-known illuminated manuscripts. A lifetime in and around the art market has taught me that there is also another whole world of manuscripts out there, which are not owned by public collections and have been seen by almost no one except their owners. There are sometimes extremely remarkable manuscripts still in private hands. Academic historians tend to overlook that most books of the late Middle Ages were originally made for individuals and for enjoyment or edification at home, alone or in shared company, and that volumes generally survived initially on domestic shelves and that they may, even now, never have been sent to libraries at all. I came to each one of the four manuscripts described here very conscious of the fact that almost no manuscript historian had seen any of these books in my lifetime. One of them had not been described from examination of the original since 1588, and the others last surfaced for public sales in 1932, 1909 and 1938, respectively. This freshness to the market is increasingly rare in our modern world.

Between them, these four manuscripts represent the cardinal points of medieval literacy. One was probably made for a woman, one for public viewing at a pilgrim shrine, one for a theologian, and one for a nobleman in the court of Burgundy. The first is a Book of Hours, the most famous and most widely-read text of the late Middle Ages, in one of the oldest known examples, and almost certainly the earliest likely to appear for sale. The second is a unique and unpublished account of the life of a woman from England in the Early Middle Ages who died as a saint in Verona, a record of oral tradition (or fiction) from the lifetime of Dante, who might actually have handled this manuscript. The third is a Latin Bible, the central text of all written knowledge in medieval Europe, in one of the most luxurious copies of its age. The last is the legend of Troy, the oldest and most

enduring war story of European history, which winds its way through the mythological foundations of Rome by Aeneas, Britain by Brutus, and Paris, of course, by Paris, all Trojans. The first manuscript is in Latin with some French, the second in Latin with Italian added, the third in Latin, and the last entirely in vernacular French. That alone epitomizes the story of language over the final two centuries of medieval Europe.

All four manuscripts, in very different ways, are richly illustrated. Between them, they have a total of 133 pictures, all described here, mostly for the first time. In every instance, we can point to other manuscripts by the artists or workshops of these books, anchoring them in a world defined by known books in public possession. In at least two of the manuscripts (possibly in all four), the illuminators were inventing subjects for the first time. Every book here would merit publication as a fine art facsimile. There are pictures in these manuscripts of kings and queens, murder, warfare, feasting, miraculous flying, singing, falling in love, travelling, dancing, playing music, marrying, hawking, playing chess, and dying — all the human joys and disasters of the romantic Middle Ages, to be held in the hands.

It may be that some of these remarkable manuscripts will pass now into institutional ownership, captured at last after lifetimes in the uncharted wild. They will become part of the public corpus of medieval books, cited and studied forever, and they will be used in their turn for defining other manuscripts as these too come to light. They will be given shelfmarks or library numbers. One or two, I secretly hope, may remain in private hands, and will stay for the next generation on the shelves and in the book cupboards of private households, to be brought out and touched and admired at home, as they always were.

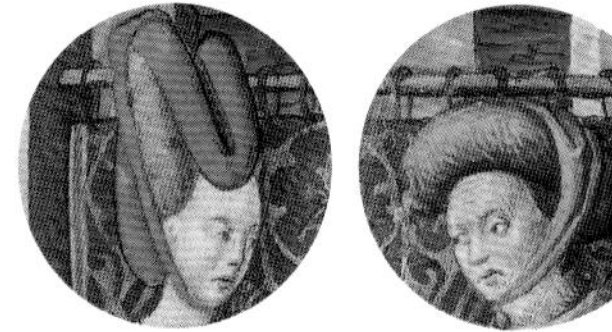

ner maximā culpā
ut de eis agam peni
nte finem meū. Amen.
rsus extracti sūt de
e magne uirtutis. Dz.
s domine cōmēdo spiri
sti me dn̄e deus ueritā
oc'los meos ne unquam
morte neq̄n dicat inimi
duersus eum. Locutus sum
eā. notū fac m̄ dn̄e finem
numerum dierum meorū quest
d desit michi. Periit fuga
requirat aīam meam. Clama
e. dixi tu es spes mea por
in uiuencium. Dirupisti

uitatorium meum
omine ad adiu
loria patri et
icut erat in
per et in secu
Alleluya.
aus tibi
nuitator
na dominu

THE HOURS OF MARIE

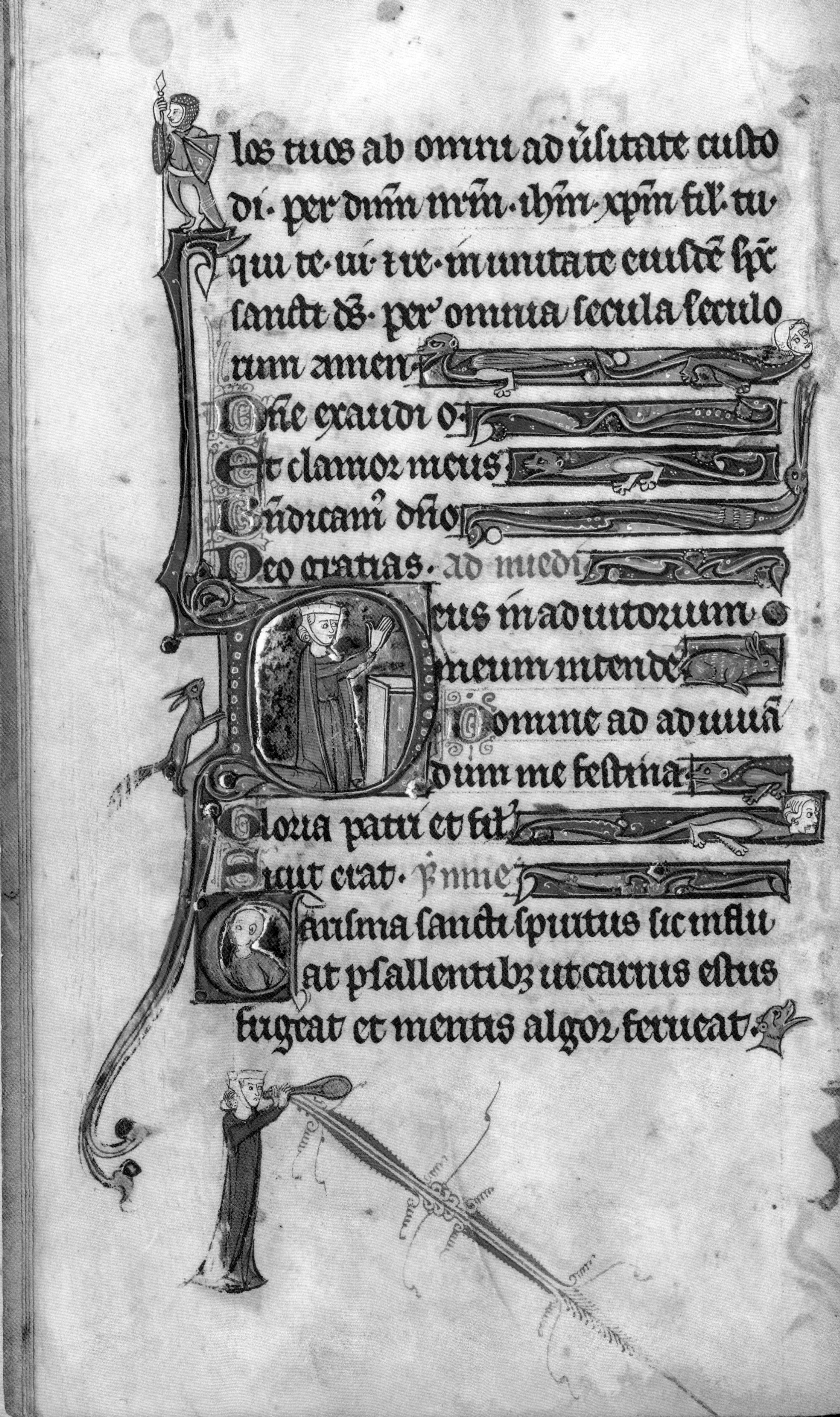

los tuos ab omni adversitate custo
di. per dnm nrm. ihm xpm fil' tu
qui tecum vi. et re. in unitate eiusdem spc
sancti ds. per omnia secula seculo
rum amen.
Dne exaudi o.
Et clamor meus
Benedicamus dno
Deo gratias. ad medi
Deus in adiutorium
meum intende.
Domine ad adiuvan
dum me festina.
Gloria patri et fil.
Sicut erat. ymne.
Carisma sancti spiritus sic influ
at psallentibus ut carnis estus
frigeat et mentis algor ferveat.

THE HOURS OF MARIE

(Use of Senlis)
In Latin and French, illuminated manuscript on parchment
Northeastern France, probably Reims, c. 1270-1280
22 historiated initials by the Reims Masters, with 2 illuminated borders
by the Master of Johannes de Phylomena

Extensively published, this is one of the oldest and most important of all early Books of Hours, and one of the few thirteenth-century books unambiguously made for a named laywoman, possibly Marie de Brabant (1256-1321), queen of France married to King Phillip III. Its pages virtually explode with a richness of imagery, in the painted initials and throughout the margins, illustrated with almost 300 images, an unusual number of which display women in daily life and are set in the royal court.

Previous page: Folios 16v-17r, a noblewoman with her daughter kneeling before the Virgin and Child enthroned
Facing page: Folio 8v, a noblewoman praying before an altar

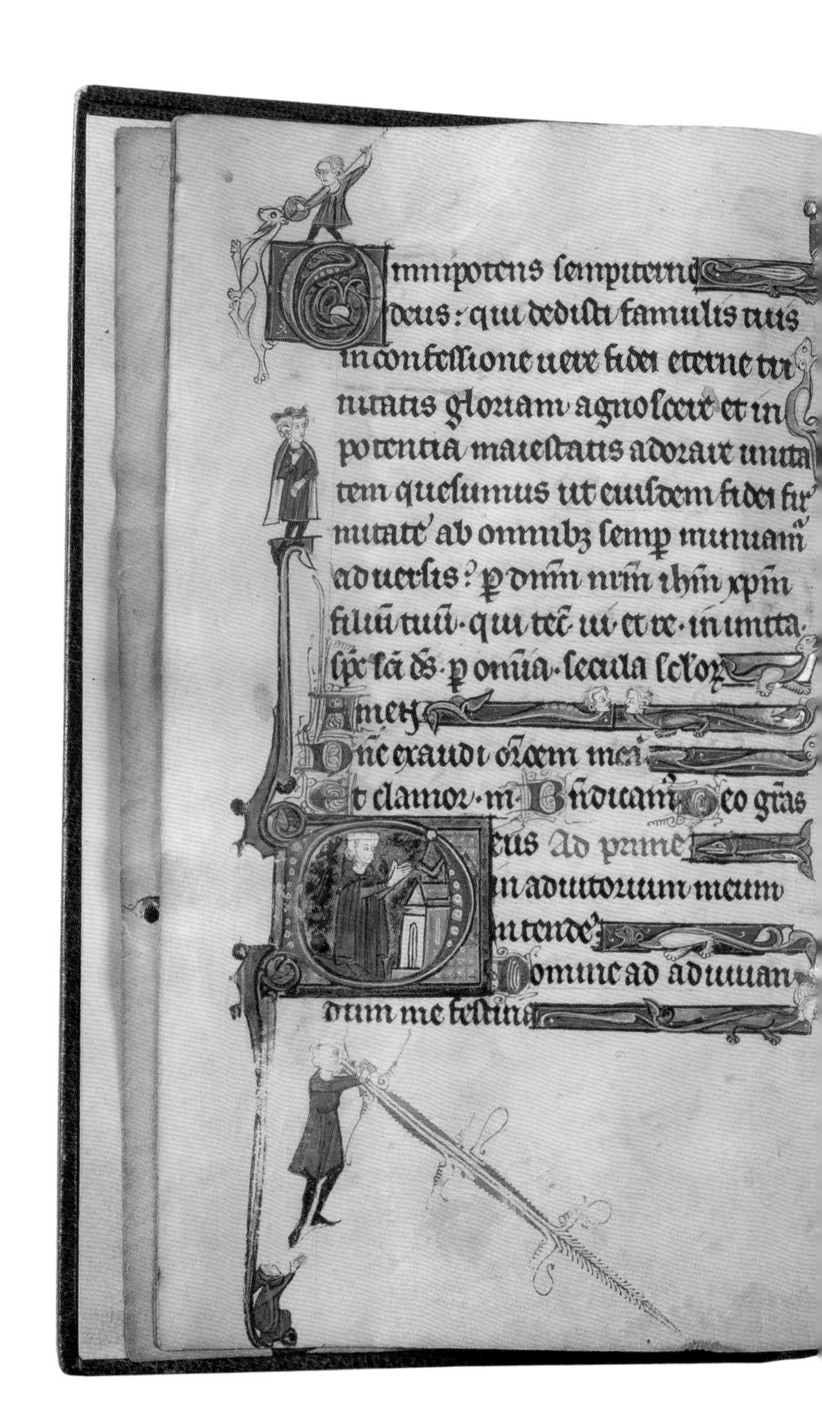
Omnipotens sempiterne
deus: qui dedisti famulis tuis
in confessione vere fidei eterne tri
nitatis gloriam agnoscere et in
potentia maiestatis adorare unita
tem quesumus ut eiusdem fidei fir
mitate ab omnibus semper muniamur
adversis. Per dominum nostrum ihesum christum
filium tuum. qui tecum vivit et regnat in unitate
spiritus sancti deus. per omnia secula seculorum.
Amen.
Domine exaudi orationem meam
Et clamor meus. Benedicamus. Deo gratias
Deus Ad prime
in adiutorium meum
intende.
Domine ad adiuvan
dum me festina.

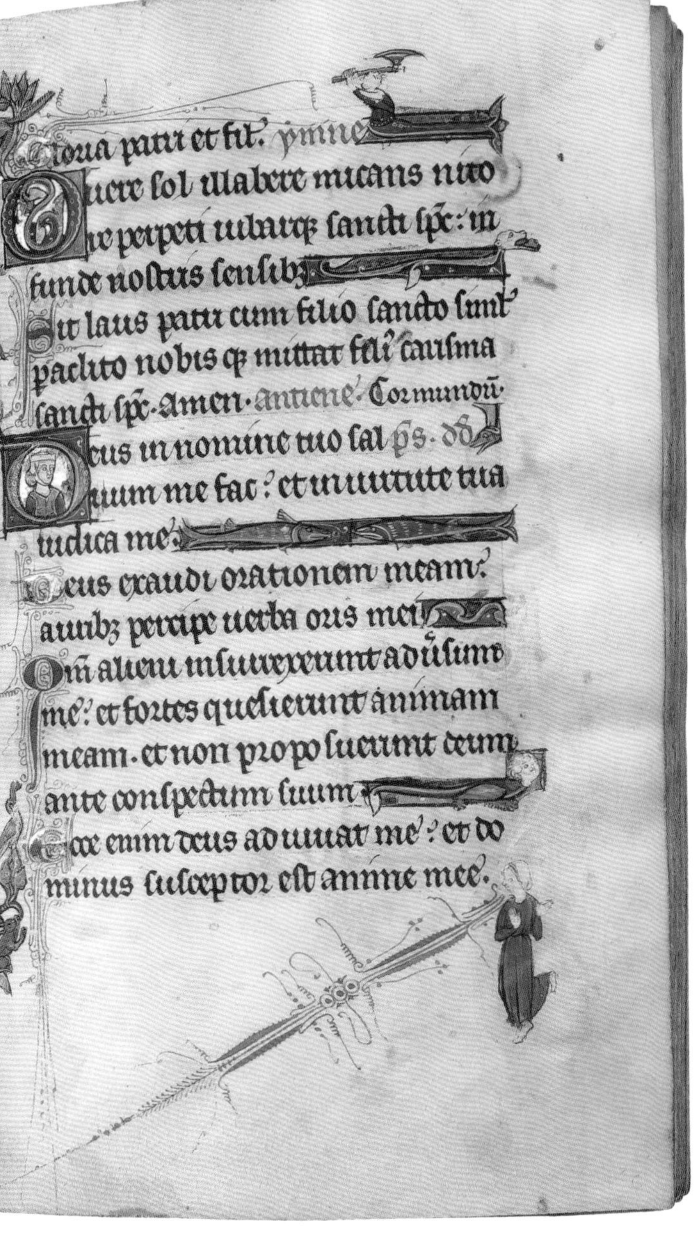

Folios 3v-4r, a noblewoman in prayer before a church

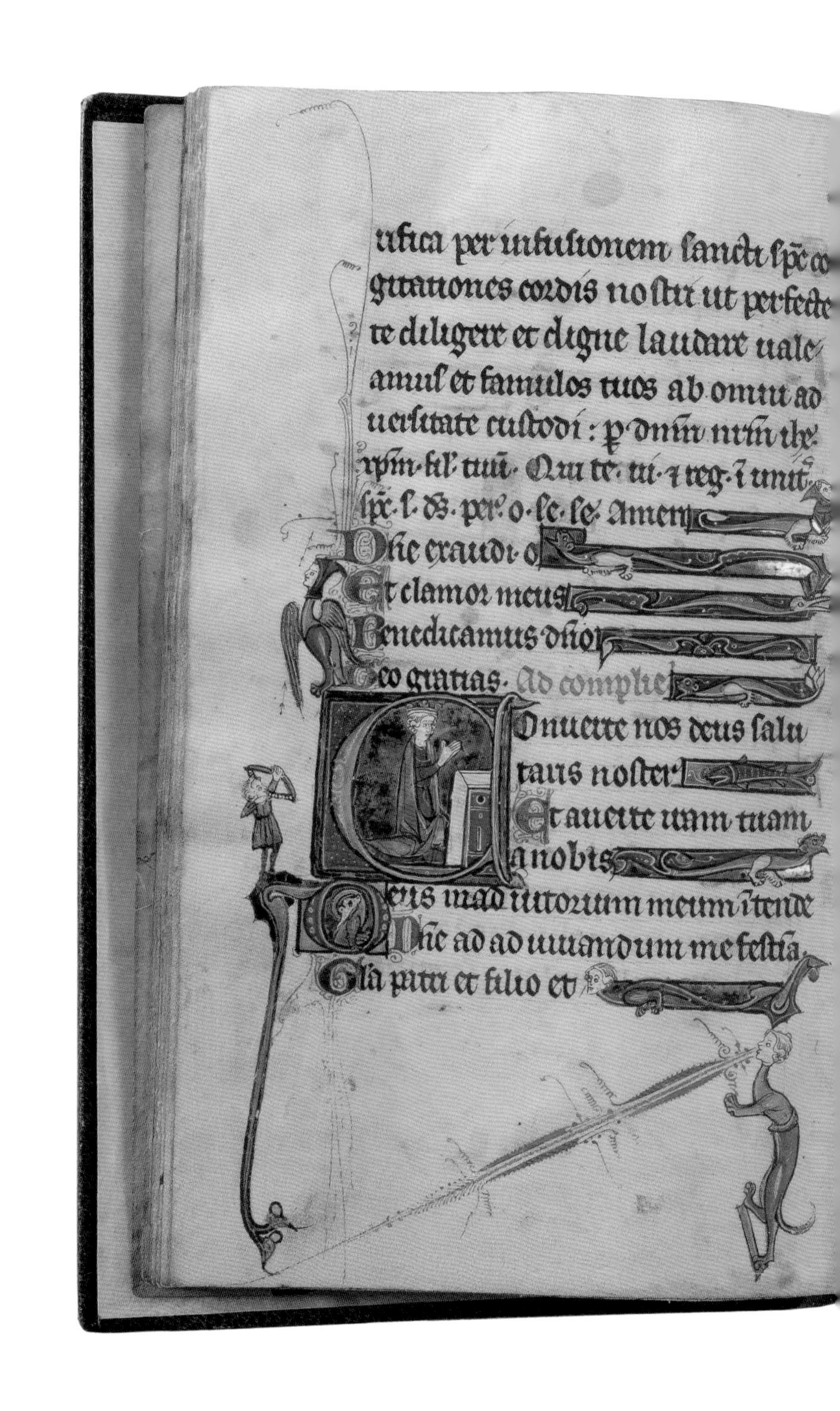

tifica per infusionem sancti spc co
gitationes cordis nostri ut perfecte
te diligere et digne laudare uale
amus et famulos tuos ab omni ad
uersitate custodi: p dnm nrm ihc
xpm fil tuu. Qui tecu uiu et reg. et unit.
spc s. ds. per o. se. se. Amen
Dne exaudi o
Et clamor meus
Benedicamus dno
Deo gratias. Ad complie
Conuerte nos deus salu
taris noster
Et auerte iram tuam
a nobis
Deus in ad iutorium meum intende
Dne ad adiuuandum me festina.
Gla patri et filio et

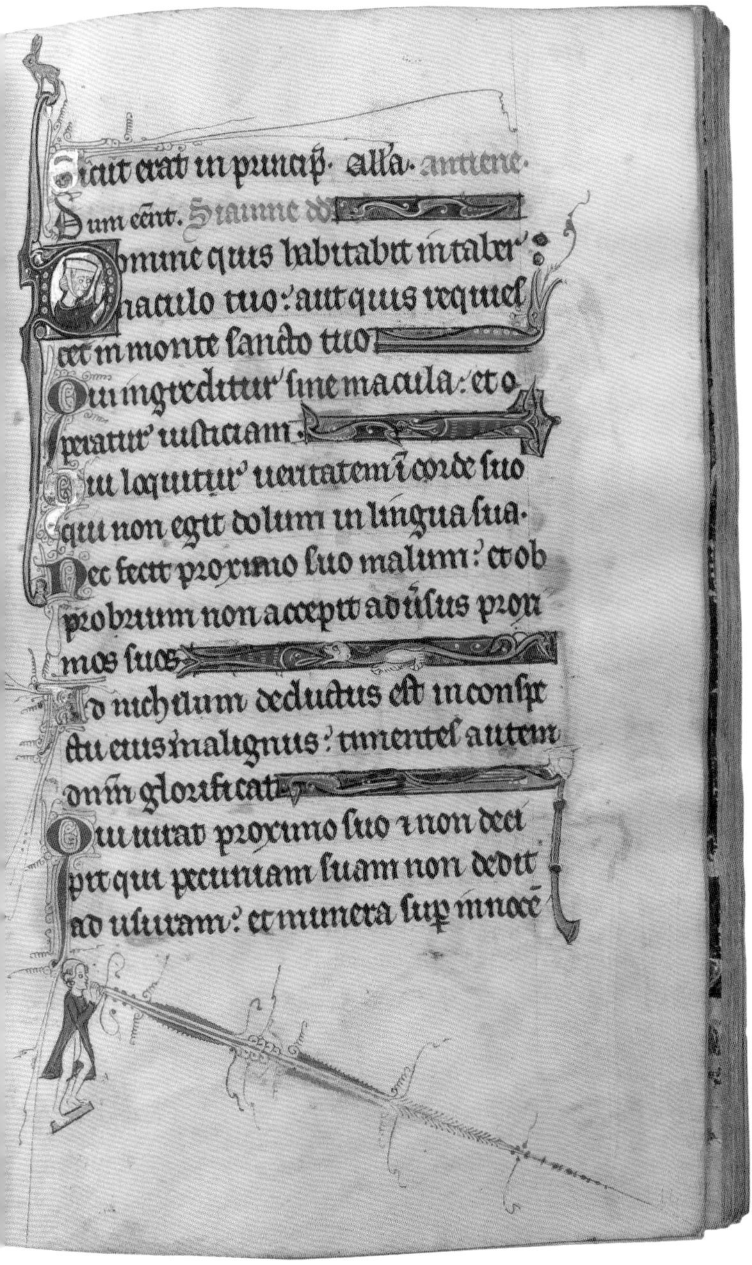
Sicut erat in principio· alla· antiene·
Domine quis habitabit in taber
naculo tuo: aut quis requiesc
et in monte sancto tuo
Qui ingreditur sine macula: et o
peratur iusticiam.
Qui loquitur ueritatem in corde suo
qui non egit dolum in lingua sua·
Nec fecit proximo suo malum: et ob
probrium non accepit adusus proxi
mos suos
Ad nichilum deductus est in conspe
ctu eius malignus: timentes autem
dominum glorificat
Qui iurat proximo suo et non deci
pit qui pecuniam suam non dedit
ad usuram: et munera super innoce

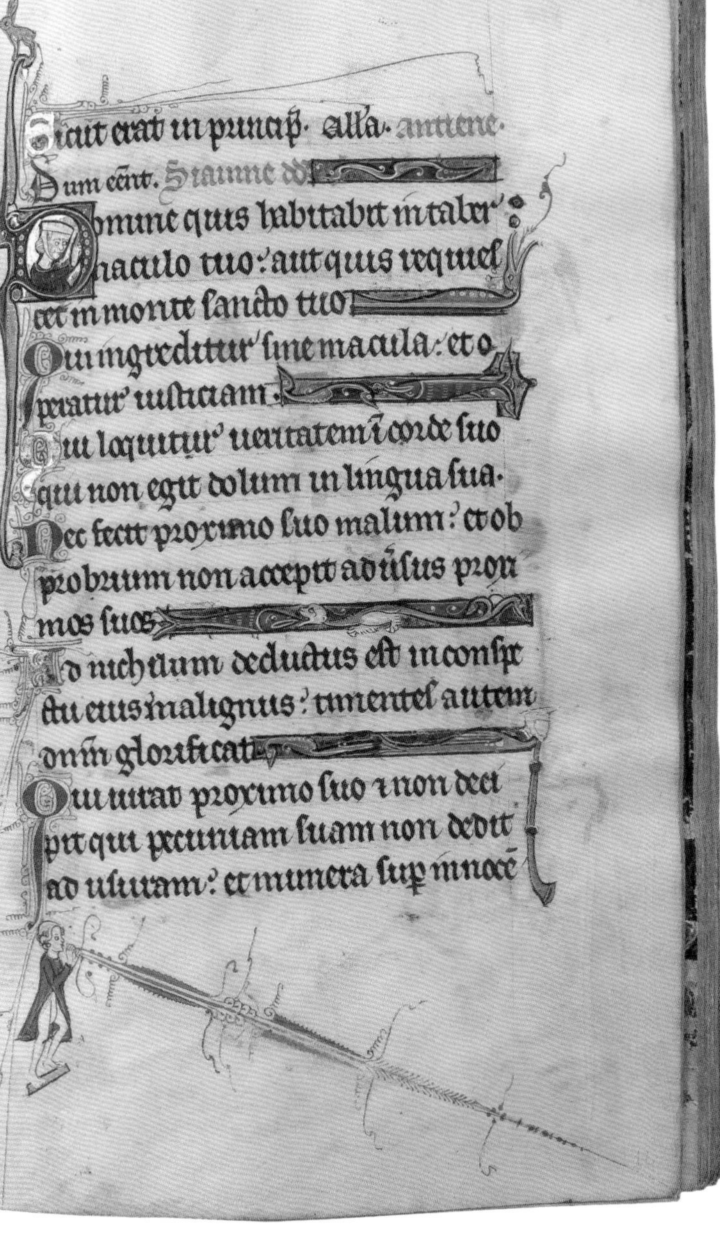

Folios 13v-14r, a king in prayer before an altar

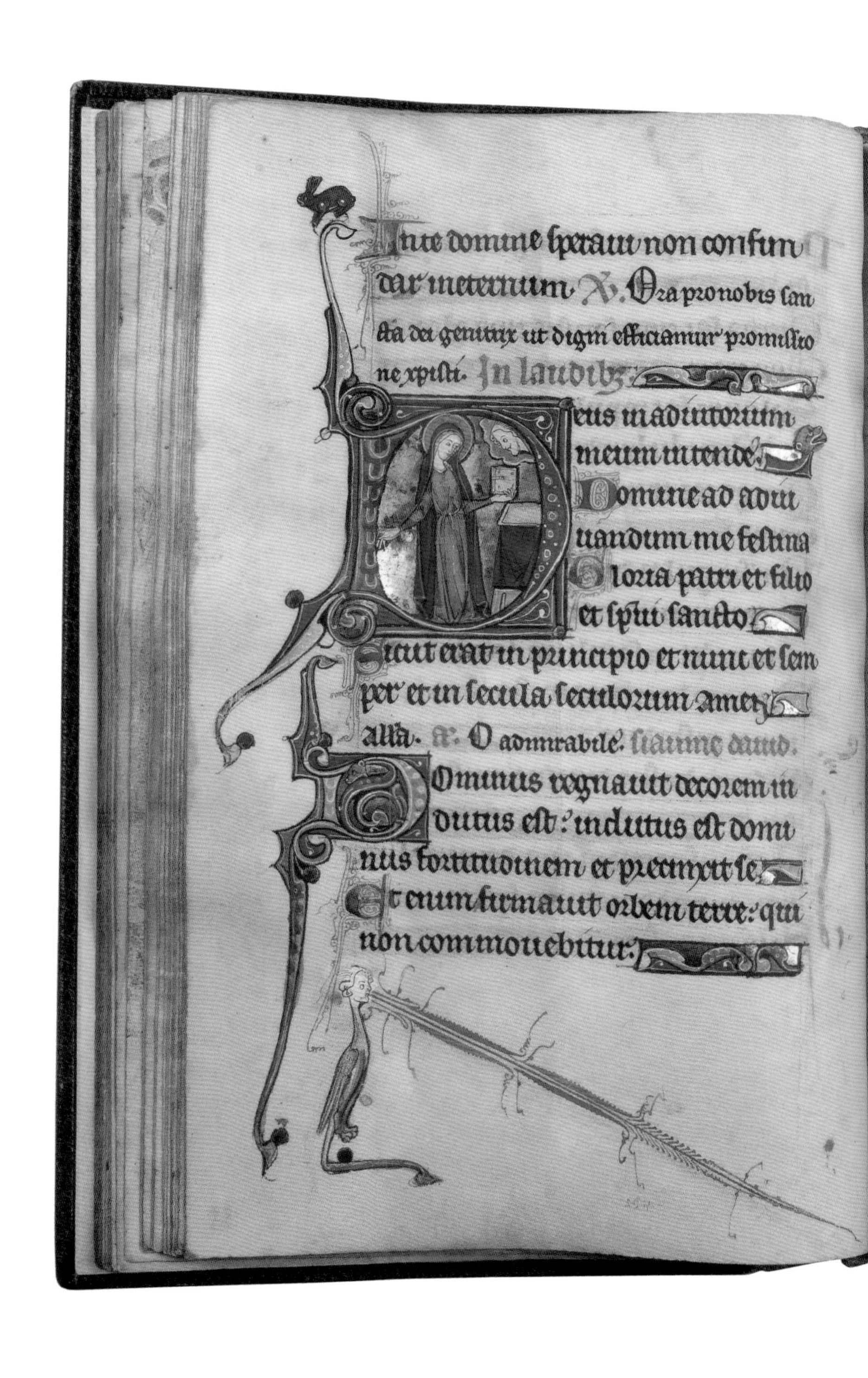

In te domine speraui non confun
dar in eternum. ℣. Ora pro nobis san
cta dei genitrix ut digni efficiamur promissio
ne xpisti. In laudibz.

Deus in adiutorium
meum intende.
Domine ad adiu
uandum me festina.
Gloria patri et filio
et spui sancto.
Sicut erat in principio et nunc et sem
per et in secula seculorum amen.
alla. A. O admirabile. psalmus dauid.

Dominus regnauit decorem in
dutus est: indutus est domi
nus fortitudinem et precinxit se.
Et enim firmauit orbem terre: qui
non commouebitur.

The Annunciation,
The Belles Heures of Jean de France, Duc de Berry,
illuminated by the Limbourg Brothers,
1405-1408/09 (New York, The Cloisters Collection,
54.1.1a, b, fol. 30r)

The first examples of Books of Hours in France began to appear as separate volumes made for lay use, often for noble women, around the second quarter of the thirteenth century. There is so far no published list, but probably about sixty French Books of Hours survive from before 1300, mostly from the last decades of the century. There may be no more than a dozen or so from as early as the third quarter. Compare that with perhaps upwards of 10,000 extant Books of Hours from the late Middle Ages, and many more among the earliest printed books. In private hands, the Hours of Marie can probably only be matched in date by a much smaller Book of Hours apparently of the Use of Troyes with 9 historiated initials (only) which was described in Les Enluminures, *An Intimate Art*, 2012, no. 1. For 15 years the Hours of Marie shared a home in the Cloisters, and often a glass case, with the *Belles Heures* of the Duc de Berry.

tetam. Amen. Memore. Sancti dei om
nes intercedite pro nostra omniumque salu
te. ℣ers. Letamini in domino et exultate iu
sti et gloriamini omnes recti corde. Orison.
Concede quesumus omnipotens
deus ut intercessio nos sancte
dei genitricis uirginis marie et o
mnium celestium uirtutum et
sanctorum patriarcharum pro
phetarum apostolorum martirum
confessorum atque sanctarum uir
ginum et omnium electorum
tuorum ubique letificet ut dum
eorum merita recolimus patroci
nia sentiamus. per eumdem do
minum nostrum ihesum xpistum
filium tuum qui tecum uiuit et
regnat in unitate spiritus sancti

Folios 42v-43r, a female saint holding out a closed book towards a young mother with a baby

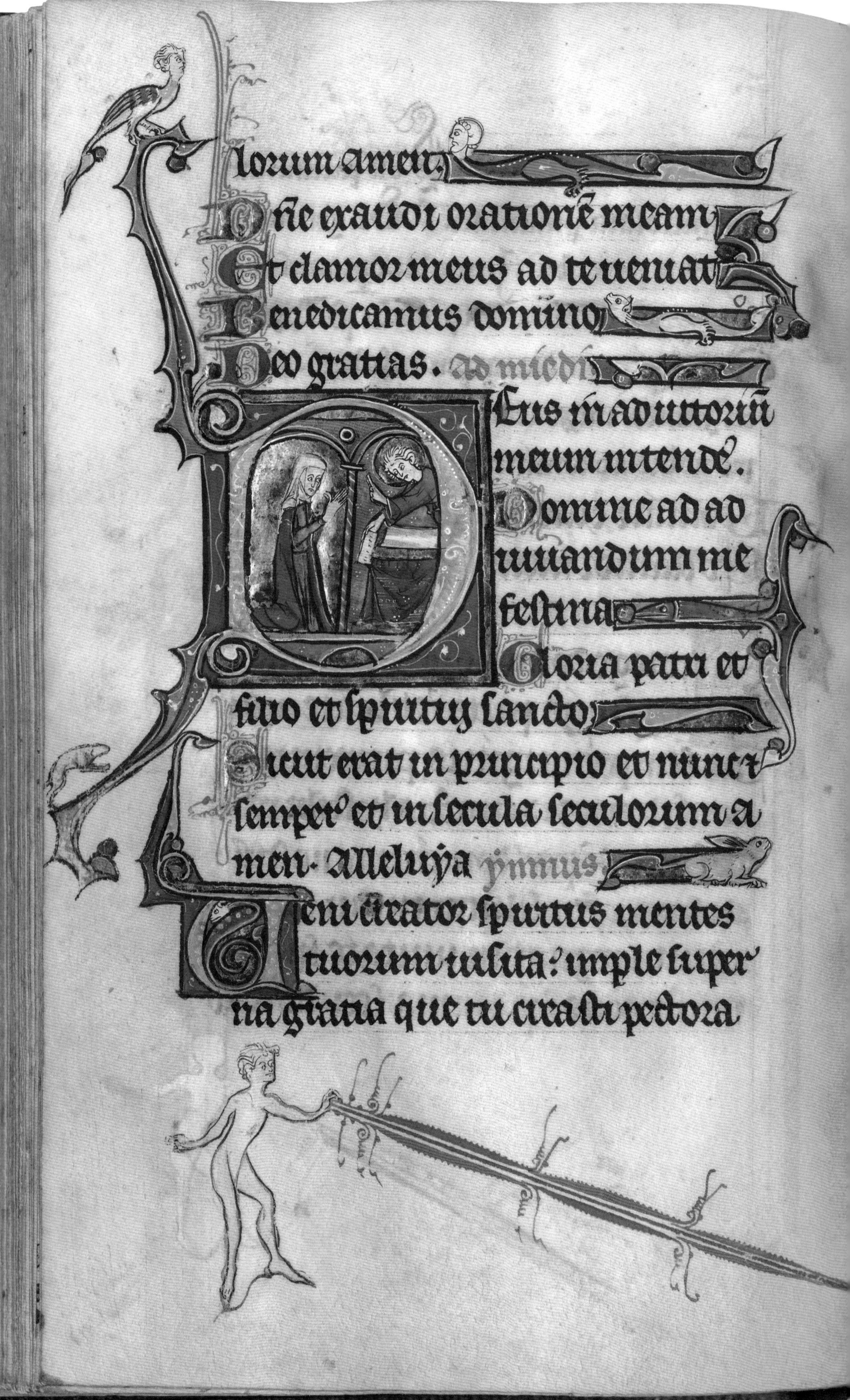

lorum amen.
Domine exaudi orationem meam
Et clamor meus ad te veniat
Benedicamus domino
Deo gratias. ad medi[am]
Deus in adiutorium
meum intende.
Domine ad ad-
iuvandum me
festina.
Gloria patri et
filio et spiritui sancto.
Sicut erat in principio et nunc et
semper et in secula seculorum a-
men. Alleluya. hymnus
Veni creator spiritus mentes
tuorum visita: imple super-
na gratia que tu creasti pectora

There are two rare and extraordinary themes in the text and decoration of the Hours of Marie. The first theme is that it is unambiguously made for female use. The origins of the literacy of women are notoriously poorly documented. "This prayerbook offers a rich yield of textual and pictorial information on the devotional practices of a woman and her family early in the reign of Philip IV" (Bennett 1996, p. 21). Many prayers are in specifically female forms (folios 176r, 200r, 205v, etc.). There are three prayers to Saint Nicholas, patron saint of young women. Bennett interprets the multiplicity of rabbits as a symbol of wishful fecundity. Very many rubrics are in French, and it is assumed that women, unlike men, were taught to read in the vernacular, itself an important stage in the development of modern languages. The manuscript may well have been an introduction for teaching Latin to a young woman. The illustrations are filled with female imagery. Fifteen of the historiated initials include or show contemporary women in daily life, either in prayer or "actively involved with religious life and family life from childhood to death" (Bennett 1996). These include the upbringing of children and the teaching of reading. There is emphasis on female saints, especially Mary Magdalen, Marie's name saint. It is assumed but very difficult to document that Books of Hours were in their origins primarily intended for women (while men used Psalters) but in no other early example is this patronage so clearly emphasized. The hundreds of border figures show a high proportion of woman involved in daily activities, including male occupations like falconry, and they conjure up an outside world very visible from a woman's perspective. The choice of text and imagery is so personalized and so unlike any other thirteenth-century Book of Hours that it is almost inconceivable that Marie herself was not involved in their selection. For the history of female literacy, spirituality and patronage of the arts in the Middle Ages, the Hours of Marie is "outstanding" (Bennett 1996).

Folio 50v, a young woman kneeling in a church while a saint appears to her and admonishes her holding a scroll

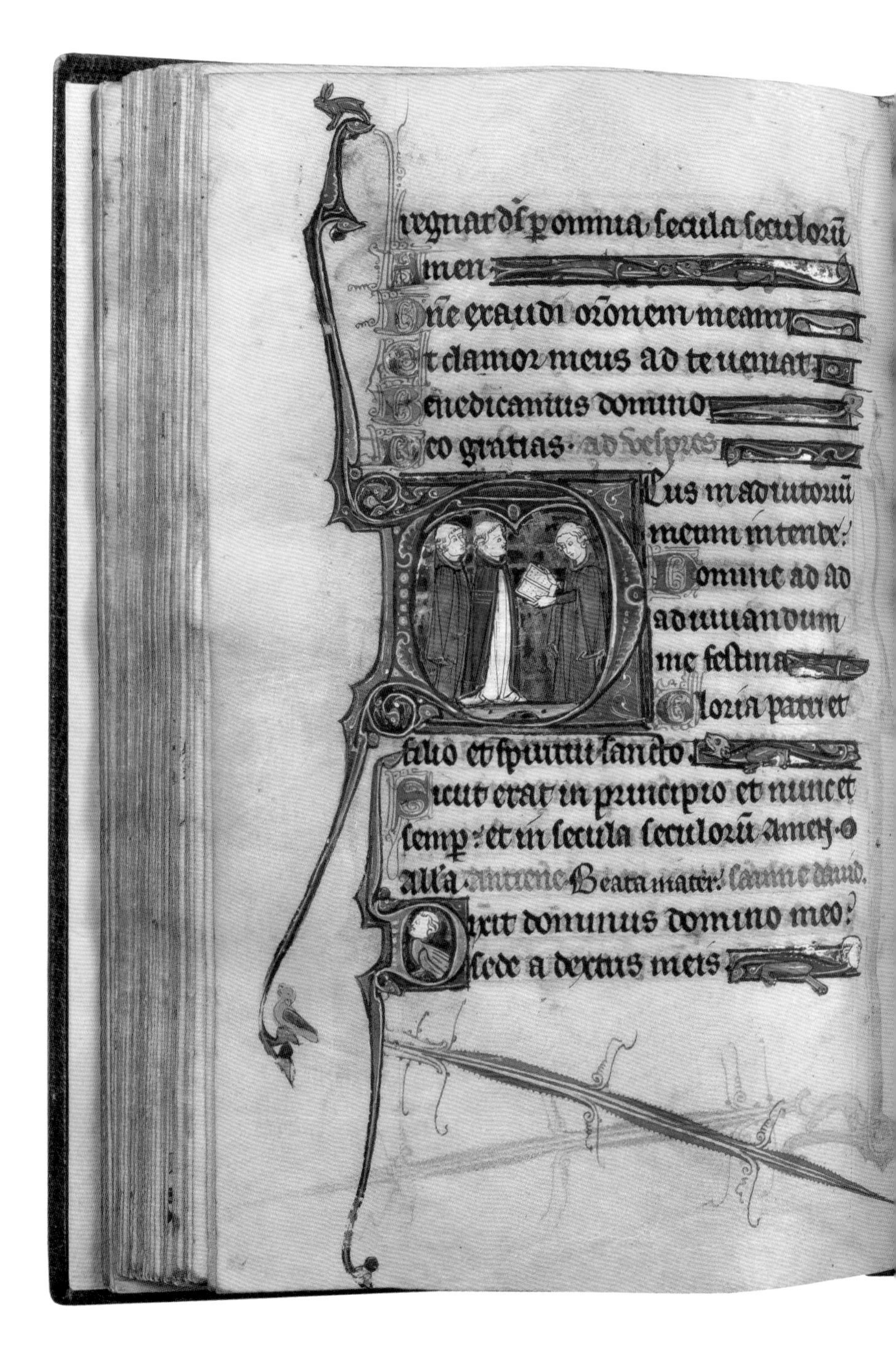

regnat ds̄ p̄ omnia secula seculorū

Amen.

Dn̄e exaudi orōnem meam.

Et clamor meus ad te veniat.

Benedicamus domino.

Deo gratias. ad vesperas

Deus in adiutoriū
meum intende.
Domine ad ad
adiuvandum
me festina.
Gloria patri et
filio et spiritui sancto.
Sicut erat in principio et nunc et
semp̄: et in secula seculorū amen. O
All'a. antiphona. Beata mater. psalmus david.
Dixit dominus domino meo:
Sede a dextris meis.

Coronation of Marie de Brabant,
Grandes Chroniques de France,
illuminated by Jean Fouquet, c. 1455-1460
(Paris, BnF, MS fr. 6465, fol. 292), detail

The second theme of the manuscript is the setting of the royal court. Whether or not Marie is to be identified with Marie of Brabant or with another woman of her circle or household, displayed prominently here are the intimate preoccupations of the period. There is a prayer on folio 87r about the Crusades, beseeching God who chose the Holy Land for our redemption to free it now from the pagans. In 1270 the future Philip III had accompanied his father Saint Louis on the Eighth Crusade. He was known as *le Hardi* from his knightly bravery in combat. The miniature along the upper margin of folio 66v shows what must be a battle in the Crusades, in which one army gallops haphazardly out of a city which seems to have a gold crescent around a spire to confront an orderly charge from a group of mounted knights encamped in a tent emblazoned with the royal fleurs-de-lys. Saint Louis died in north Africa on 25 August, whereupon Philip was proclaimed king of France; his first wife died soon after and Philip arrived back in France as a widower. The miniature on folio 96r shows a death bed, and there is a queen with downturned eyes in the adjacent margin.

Folio 56v, a young man, perhaps at school or university, wearing a red robe and holding a book, being addressed by a priest and master in a brown habit

Undoubtedly the book was written for female use for a woman called Marie, who is named in a prayer to God at the top of folio 198v, "famula tua maria" – "your servant Marie"– probably the earliest extant Book of Hours made for any patron mentioned by name in the text. She is frequently shown in the miniatures kneeling in prayer, twice as a queen wearing a golden crown (folios 1r and 7r). The kneeling figure on folio 13v is a king. Crowned queens occur commonly as marginal figures, including facing the death scene (folios 93v-94r) and on the last full page of text. One vignette shows a king of France fighting in the Crusades (folio 66v) and the text includes a crusader prayer (folio 87r). The Use is that of Senlis, north east of Paris, and invocations of saints suggest connections both with the court of Paris and the southern Netherlands. The artist, however, probably worked in Reims, east of Senlis, metropolitan capital of the Church in France. The likelihood is that the manuscript was made for an intimate of the court of Philip III of France (r. 1270-1285), a crusader, who was crowned in Reims Cathedral on 30 August 1271. The first page, which is missing, would have contained any coats-of-arms.

As already mentioned, a possibility has to be that this was the Book of Hours of Marie de Brabant (1256-1321), queen of France, who married Philip III at the age of 18 on 21 August 1274. The date would fit the artistic style, as would the liturgical blend and the emphasis on queens and the hoped-for fecundity of a young bride. Marie's eventual children were the count of Évreux and the future queens of Bohemia and England. She was an ancestor of the Duc de Berry, Jeanne d' Évreux, Jeanne de Navarre, and other great patrons of the early royal Books of Hours of the fourteenth century.

The Annunciation, *Psalter* (Reims Psalter), c. 1275-80? (London, BL, Add. MS 17868, fol. 14v)

Folio 62r, a young woman kneeling behind a priest who reads from a book on a lectern watched by an older woman, probably her mother, from the lower margin

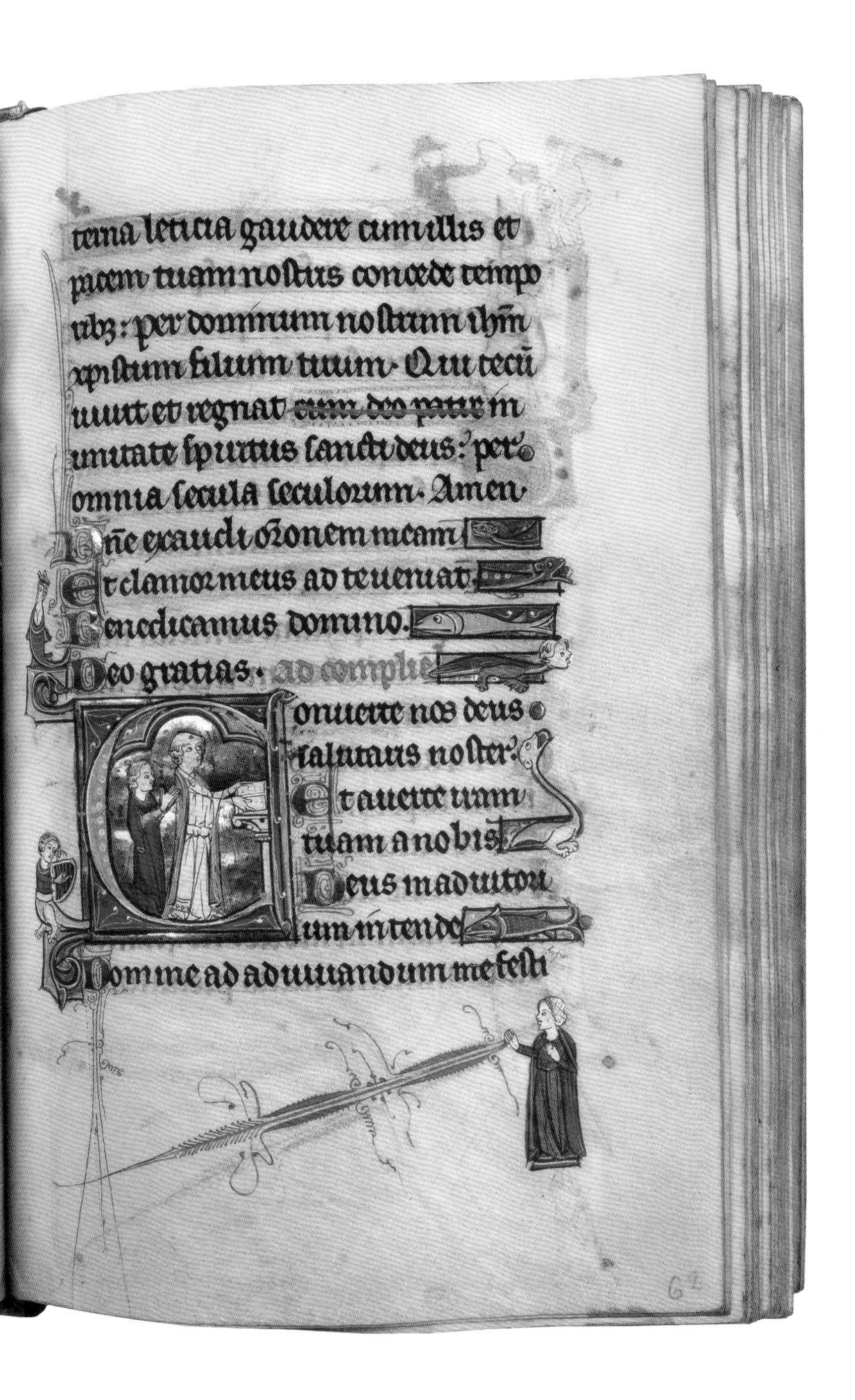
terna leticia gaudere cum illis et
pacem tuam nostris concede tempo
ribȝ: per dominum nostrum ihm̄
xpistum filium tuum. Qui tecū
uiuit et regnat cum deo patre in
unitate spiritus sancti deus: per
omnia secula seculorum. Amen
Dn̄e exaudi oronem meam
Et clamor meus ad te ueniat
Benedicamus domino.
Deo gratias. ad complet
Conuerte nos deus
salutaris noster.
Et auerte iram
tuam a nobis
Deus in adiutori
um meum intende
Domine ad adiuuandum me festi

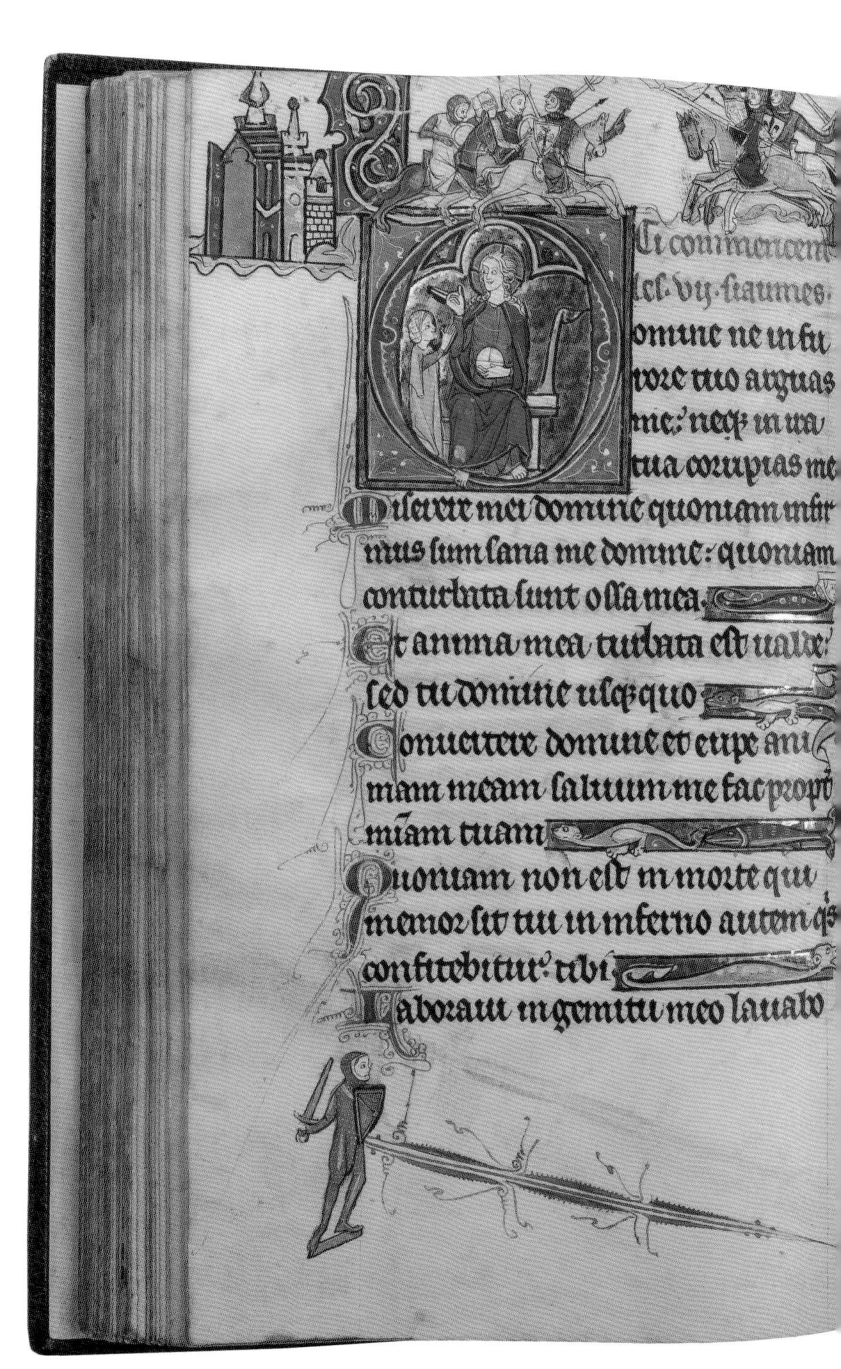

Ci commencent
les .vij. siaumes.
Domine ne in fu
rore tuo arguas
me: neque in ira
tua corripias me.
Miserere mei domine quoniam infir
mus sum sana me domine: quoniam
conturbata sunt ossa mea.
Et anima mea turbata est valde:
sed tu domine usque quo
Convertere domine et eripe ani
mam meam salvum me fac propter
misericordiam tuam
Quoniam non est in morte qui
memor sit tui in inferno autem quis
confitebitur tibi
Laboravi in gemitu meo lavabo

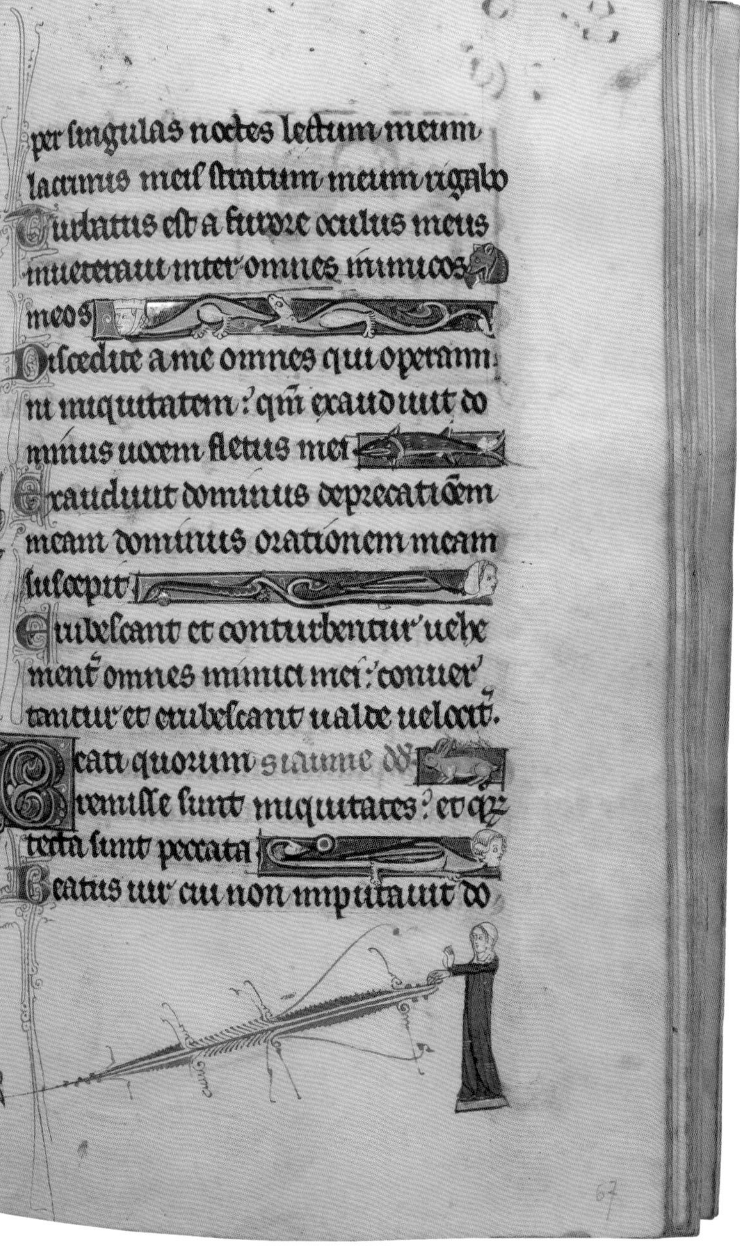

Folios 66v-67r, a woman in prayer before Christ enthroned and blessing her with vignette along the upper margin showing a battle in the Crusades

View of Reims Cathedral, west façade, 13th century, or c. 1255-1274

The manuscript is of astounding richness. Every page is glitteringly illuminated, generally with elaborate initials and line-fillers incorporating human and animal forms and displays of firework penwork. The principal artist of the miniatures, like the text, draws extensively from Parisian models in the style of the so-called "Bari" workshop in the 1250s and 1260s, named after a Gradual now in a church in Bari, probably made in the royal *capella* in Paris. The figure style includes the long-arched noses characteristic of that style, and colors resembling stained glass windows backlit by sunlight. However, the work here points to execution in northeastern France. The choice of antiphons in the text is that identified later as being of the Use of Senlis, although it is not clear how precisely usage is localizable to place of production in the thirteenth century.

The closest consistent parallels are with illumination in Reims, seat of the metropolitan archdiocese, and Alison Stones describes the painter of the Hours of Marie as a "Reims Master." There is a close kinship with the presumed Reims Psalter in the British Library,

Folio 75r, Saint Francis kneeling in prayer before a church or hermitage

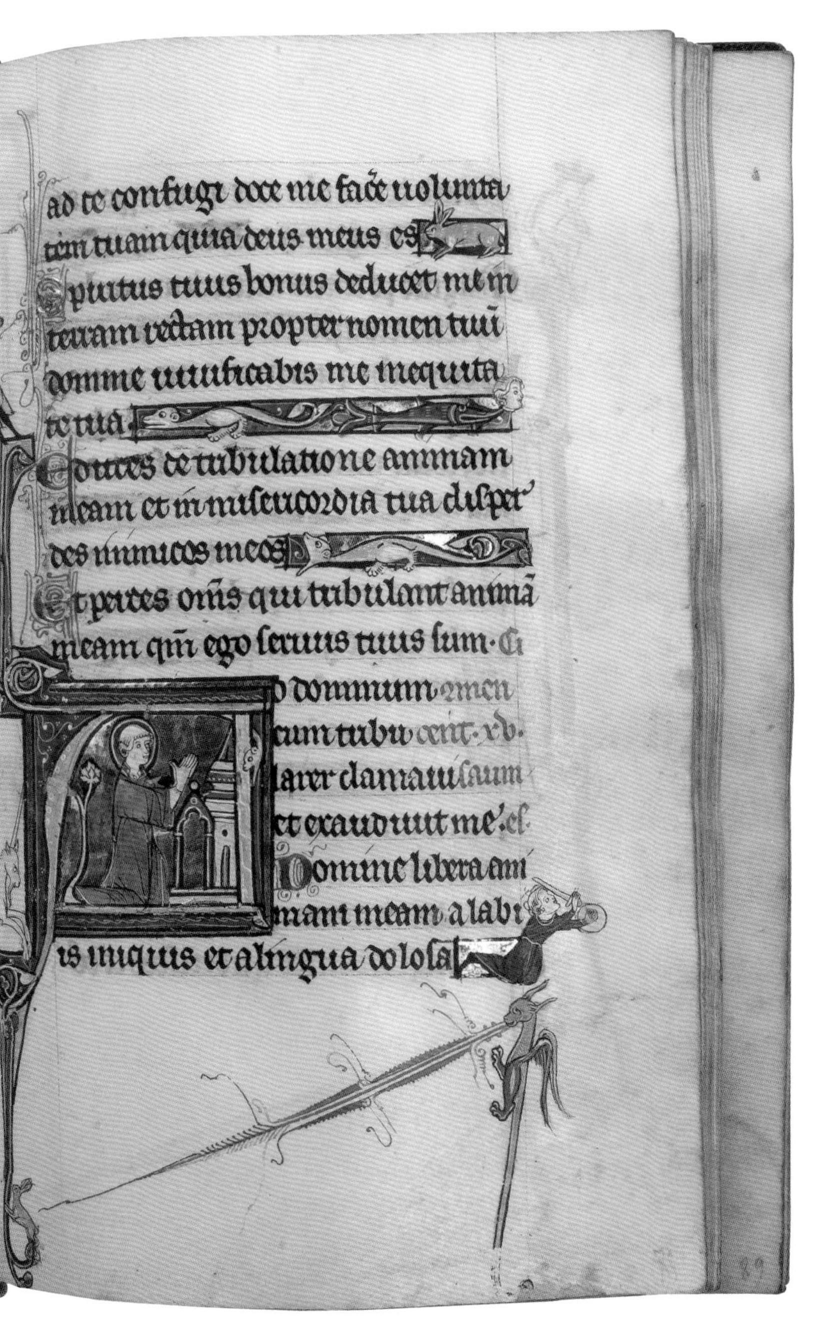

ad te confugi doce me facere volunta
tem tuam quia deus meus es
Spiritus tuus bonus deducet me in
terram rectam propter nomen tuum
domine vivificabis me in equita
te tua
Educes de tribulatione animam
meam et in misericordia tua disper
des inimicos meos
Et perdes omnes qui tribulant animam
meam quoniam ego servus tuus sum. G
Ad dominum
cum tribu
larer clamavi
et exaudivit me.
Domine libera ani
mam meam a labi
is iniquis et a lingua dolosa

Add. MS 17868, which also shows dependence on earlier Parisian designs. Reims Cathedral is one of the greatest of all thirteenth-century buildings and the city was a notable focus for artists. This was probably a workshop rather than the hand of a single illuminator. The use of gold in the initials on folios 34v and 53v is different, within a consistent style. The oddity is in the two relatively minor initials on folios 146v-147r including little men in prayer and dragons with large wings of extraordinary splendor. These are by an artist who worked in Cambrai, known as the Master of Johannes de Phylomena, from an Evangeliary in Cambrai, signed by a scribe of that name (Bibliothèque municipale, MSS 189-90).

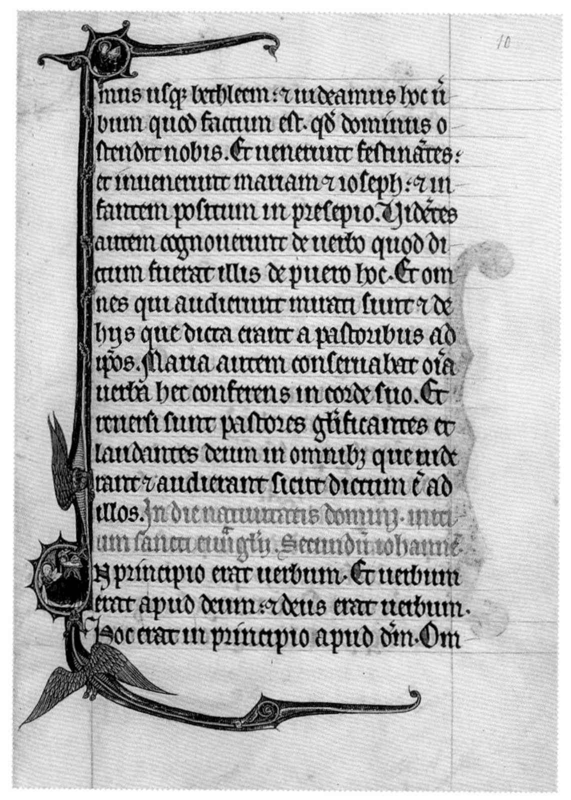

Evangeliary of the Cathedral of Cambrai, illuminated border by the Master of Johannes de Phylomena, c. 1266 (Cambrai, Bibliothèque municipale, MS 189, fol. 10)

In addition to the larger initials, the manuscript has an almost unparalleled richness of minor decoration, filling and supplementing the text. Adelaide Bennett writes: "Until now, no other contemporary French manuscript – Parisian or from the northeast – has prepared us for the virtual explosion of coordinated penwork and imagery in the margins of Marie's book" (Bennett 1996, p. 24). The sale catalogue of 1932 counted 280 illustrated scenes or figures in the borders. The margins are filled too with sparkling color: "astonishing penwork sprays resemble sparks, often converging toward the gutter of the book" (Bennett 1996, p. 24).

PHYSICAL DESCRIPTION

Parchment flyleaf + 209 folios on parchment (5 originally blank) + parchment flyleaf, lacking at least 6 leaves at beginning and 3 blanks elsewhere, else complete, first two surviving leaves bound in reverse order, modern pencil foliation (followed here) begins with '5' on the third leaf but repeats '159' and '187' and so reaches '[209]' by the end, collation: i2 [doubtless of 8, lacking i-vi, vii-viii bound in reverse order], ii8, iii4 [iv originally blank], iv-xii8, xiii5 [of 6, blank vi cancelled], xiv-xx8, xxi4 [iii-iv originally blank], xxii-xxiv8, xxv6 [of 8, blank i-ii cancelled], xxvi-xxviii8, xxix4 [iii-iv blank], with one remaining catchword (folio 72v, end of quire x); ruled in plummet, justification 112 x 70 mm., single column, 18 lines, written in dark brown ink in two sizes of a gothic hand or *littera textualis* beginning below top line, rubrics in red; line-fillers throughout in burnished gold with colors and white tracery in myriads of designs including people, fish, dragons, birds, animals, monsters, grotesques, some naturalistic, many very comic; one-line versal initials throughout alternately blue with red penwork or burnished gold with dark blue penwork; firework bursts of diagonal penwork in the lower margins throughout in red and blue; 2-line illuminated initials throughout in elaborate leafy designs in colors and burnished gold often enclosing or including dragons and other creatures including human heads and with scrolling marginal extensions, often supporting birds and animals; marginal figures throughout including men and women in numerous poses, dancing, hunting, fighting, praying and clambering through the foliage and penwork sprays (see below); twenty-two historiated initials from 3 to 9 lines high in colors with white tracery and highly burnished gold grounds and usually long scrolling marginal extensions; once-wide margins cropped with some loss of extremities of figures or scenes in the upper and sometimes outer borders, some smudging and thumbing affecting the illumination, some staining and cockling especially towards the end, a picture or other piece once pasted on folio 153v now removed; nineteenth-century French blind-stamped binding by Gruel (signed in gilt at foot of spine), parchment endleaves, gilt edges, in a full black morocco fitted case. Dimensions 173 x 116 mm.

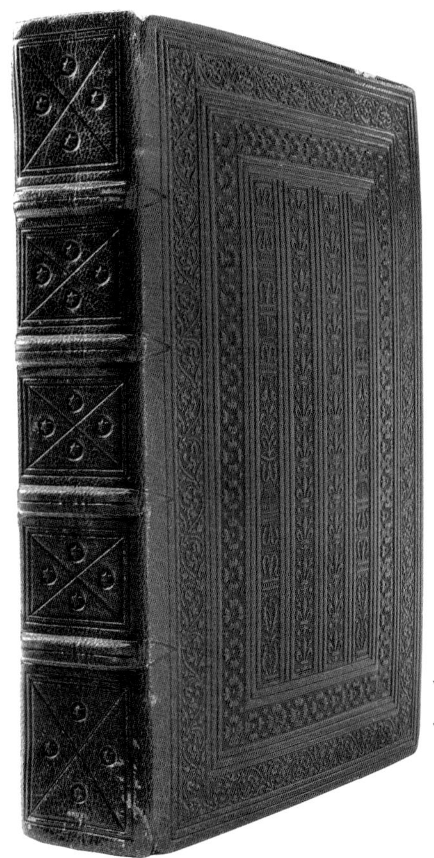

reduced

The Hours of Marie, binding

TEXT

ff. 1r-15r, the Hours of the Holy Ghost, comprising one remaining leaf of Matins (folio [2]), and Lauds (ff. [1] and 5r-v), Prime (ff. 5v-7r), Terce (ff. 7r-8v), Sext (ff. 8v-10r), None (ff. 10r-11v), Vespers (ff. 11v-13v) and Compline (ff. 13v-15r); ff. 15v-16v are prayers and verses from psalms added in the fifteenth century;

ff. 17r-66r, the Hours of the Virgin, Use consistent with Senlis, comprising Matins (ff. 17r-34v), Lauds (ff. 34v-43r), Prime, with antiphon *O admirabile* and capitulum *Hec est virgo*

qui lapsorum sublevator inenarrabi
lis fac nos famulos tuos sancte dei ge
nitricis virginis marie et omnium
sanctorum tuorum ubique tueri presidi
is nec non familiaritate atque consan
guinitate nobis coniunctis et omni
populo christiano cunctis insidiis fal
lacis inimici depulsis concede ad ce
lestem patriam redeundi aditum ac
defunctorum omnium fidelium sa
cri baptismatis unda renatorum a
nimabus quiete perfrui sempiterna.
Per eundem dominum nostrum ihesum christum

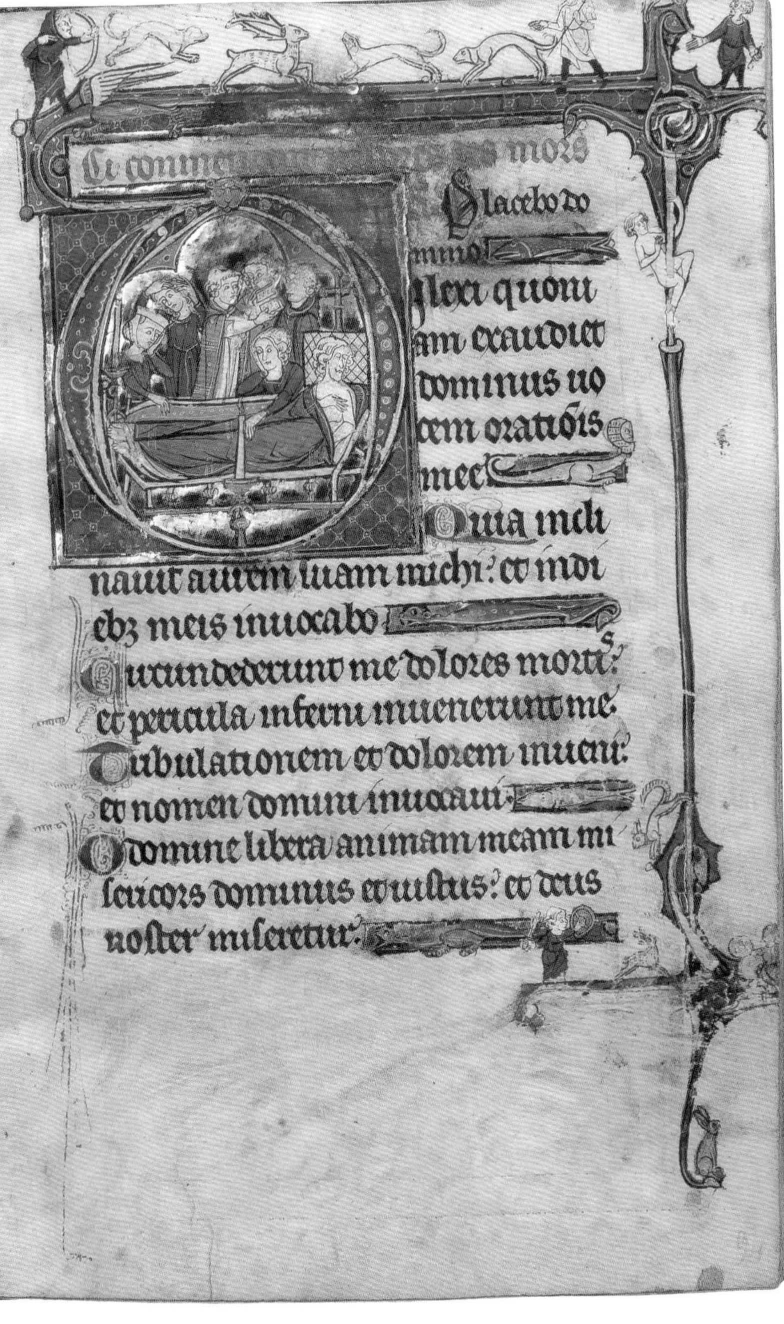

Folios 93v-94r, a death scene, a man lying in bed attended by his wife and (probably) son, with another woman tearing at her hair and two priests and a figure behind who seems to be wearing a crown

(ff. 43v-47r), Terce (ff. 47r-50v), Sext (ff. 50v-53v), None, with antiphon *Germinavit* and capitulum *Per te dei* (53v-56v), Vespers (ff. 56v-62r) and Compline (ff. 62r-66r);

ff. 66v-93v, Psalms, prayers and Litany, comprising the Penitential Psalms (folios 66v-75r); the Gradual Psalms, with Athanasian Creed and other prayers (ff. 87r-97r), including a prayer specifically about the Crusades ("Deus qui ad redemptionis ...," folio 87r, see above); and Litany (ff. 87r-93v), including Saints Denis, Irenaeus, Firminus, Germanus, Remigius, Columbanus and Columba, with further prayers and petitions;

ff. 94r-151v, the Office of the Dead, Use of Senlis, comprising Vespers (ff. 94r-100v) including a collect for use by a woman against the plague; and Matins (ff. 100v-120r) and Lauds (ff. 120r-131v), followed by collects, including another for female use; the Commendation of Souls, psalms "*que on dit ou servige des mors*" (ff. 131v-151v), with further collects; folio 152r with a prayer added in the fifteenth century; ff. 152v-153v blank;

ff. 154r-173r, Suffrages, prayers, canticles and psalms, comprising 40 suffrages (*les memoires des sains et des saintes*) to be used at Matins, Prime or Vespers (ff. 154r-170r), including Saints Victor, Denis, Cyriacus, Blaise, Thomas Becket, Nicasius (of Reims), Francis, Eligius, Fiacre, Suplicius, Germanus, and Geneviève, leaving blank pages to allow for any subsequent additions in the categories of apostles, martyrs, confessors and virgins (ff. 157v-158r, 161v, 165r-v and 168v), followed by other prayers for peace and Saint Leonard (patron of prisoners); a canticle and other psalms (ff. 170r-173v), including prayers for Saints Lupus and Theobald; and the Litany of the Virgin (ff. 173r-176v), with folio 177r left blank for any additions;

ff. 177v-207r, the Mass of the Virgin (ff. 177v-197v), with rubrics in French, followed by personal prayers, "*les grans orisons en latin et en francois*" (ff. 198r-207r), for female use, to God, against adversity, and to the Virgin and to Saints John the Evangelist, Mary Magdalen and Nicholas; ff. 207v-[209v] blank;

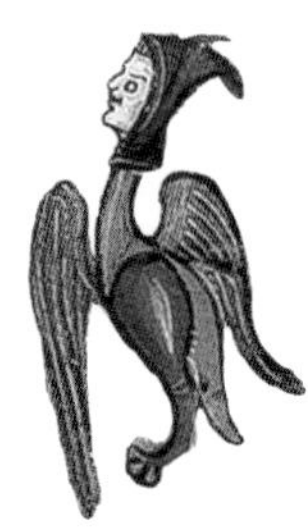

ILLUMINATION

The historiated initials are:

1. Folio 1r, A queen praying at an altar, historiated initial, 3 lines.

2. Folio 3v, A noblewoman in prayer before a church, 4 lines.

3. Folio 7r, A queen praying at an altar, 4 lines.

4. Folio 8v, A noblewoman praying before an altar, 4 lines.

5. Folio 10r, A young woman in prayer before a church, 4 lines.

6. Folio 11v, A noblewoman praying before an altar, 4 lines.

7. Folio 13v, A king in prayer before an altar, 4 lines.

8. Folio 17r, A noblewoman with her daughter kneeling before the Virgin and Child enthroned, 9 lines, within an elaborate border including a hunter with hounds chasing

a hare, a piebald musician with a viol, a tournament with three galloping knights and two fighting solders judged by a woman with banners and watched by other women on the battlements of a castle.

9. Folio 22r, Saint Peter seated on a bench, 4 lines.

10. Folio 34v, A female saint holding out a closed book over an altar as God appears to her from the sky, 6 lines, "perhaps this is an annunciation of the parturition, to be realized in the following initial" (Bennett 1996, p. 26).

11. Folio 43r, A female saint holding out a closed book towards a young mother with a baby, 6 lines, "quite unusual … The mother in intimate contact with her infant demonstrates her very human concern for parenting – nurturing and caring for her child" (ibid., Bennett 1996).

12. Folio 47r, A woman seated with a book addressing a young man standing beside her, 6 lines, "suggests a household scene of a mother educating her son" (ibid., Bennett 1996).

13. Folio 50v, A young woman kneeling in a church while a saint appears to her and admonishes her holding a scroll, 6 lines. The naked man in the margin "may be apotropaic, protecting against dangers of lust and sexuality" (Bennett 1996, p. 27).

14. Folio 53v, A young woman kneeling in prayer, with Christ appearing to her, 6 lines.

15. Folio 56v, A young man, perhaps at school or university, wearing a red robe and holding a book, being addresed by a priest and master in a brown habit, 6 lines.

16. Folio 62r, A young woman kneeling behind a priest who reads from a book on a lectern, 6 lines, watched by an older woman, probably her mother, from the lower margin.

17. Folio 66v, A woman in prayer before Christ enthroned and blessing her, 6 lines, with vignette along the upper margin showing a battle in the Crusades, with Saracens galloping out from a city with a gold crescent on a tower to confront a Christian army led by a king and knights with a fleur-de-lys on a shield, as a trumpter stands outside their tent emblazoned with fleurs-de-lys.

18. Folio 75r, Saint Francis kneeling in prayer before a church or hermitage, 6 lines, with a unicorn in the margin beside him.

19. Folio 94r, A death scene, a man lying in bed attended by his wife and (probably) son, with another woman tearing at her hair and two priests and a figure behind who seems to be wearing a crown, 8 lines, upper margin including a hunting scene with an archer shooting a stag cornered by hounds.

20. Folio 105v, A priest reading a lection in the Office of the Dead, 3 lines.

21. Folio 186r, A woman kneeling in prayer before an altar, with Christ appearing to her, 4 lines.

22. Folio 198r, A young woman kneeling with her priest at an altar, 3 lines.
There are 2-line historiated initials showing heads of women (including folios 11r, 12r, 12v, 14r, 25r, 31r, 35v, 43r, 50r, 82v, 93r, 95v, 99v, 131r, 155v, 159v, 160r, 164r and 182v) and occasionally showing men (such as 44r, 49v – a knight – 104r, 158v and 162r). The marginal figures and grotesques include queens, one reaching up to a bird (folios 2v, 58r,

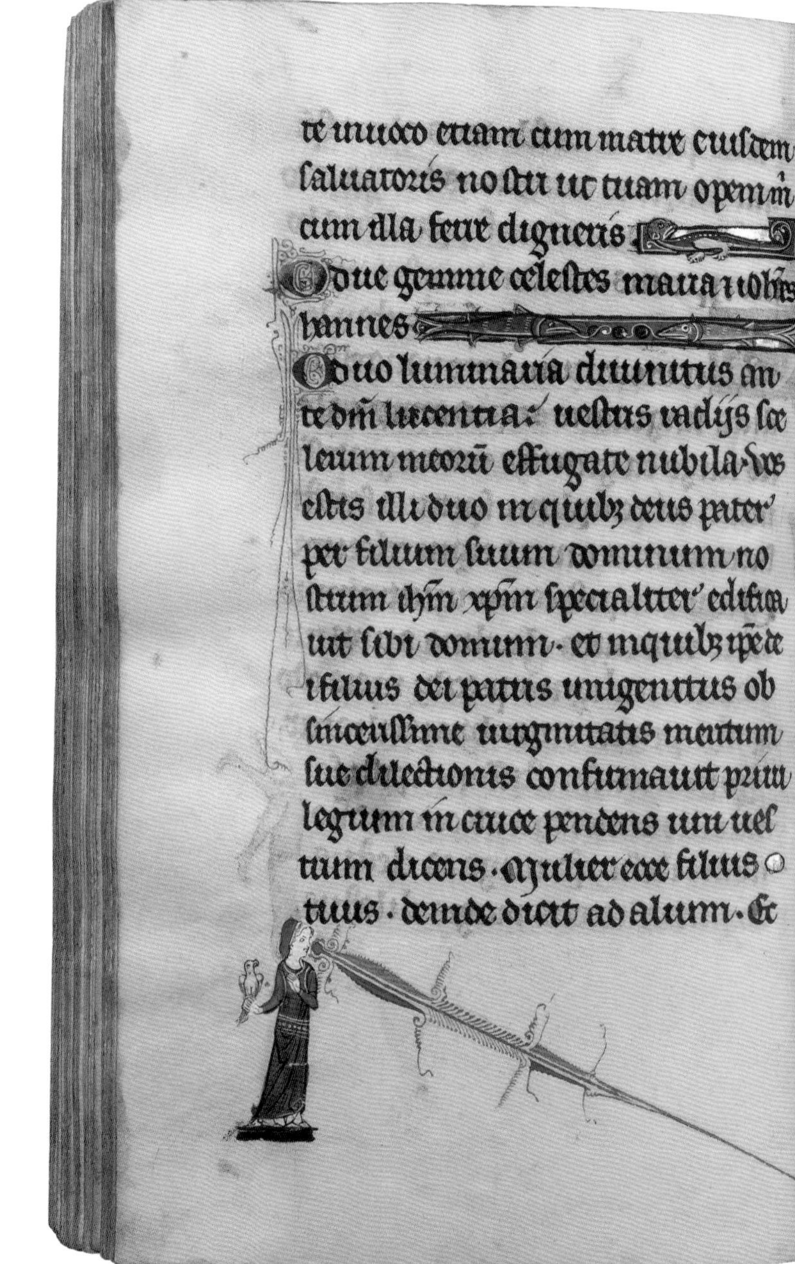

te inuoco etiam cum matre eiusdem
saluatoris nostri ut tuam opem in
cum illa ferre digneris.
O due gemme celestes maria et io
hannes
O duo luminaria diuinitus an
te dm̄ lucentia: uestris radijs sce
lerum meorū effugate nubila. Vos
estis illi duo in quibꝫ deus pater
per filium suum dominum no
strum ihm̄ xp̄m specialiter edifica
uit sibi domum. et in quibꝫ ipse
filius dei patris unigenitus ob
sincerissime uirginitatis meritum
sue dilectionis confirmauit priui
legium in cruce pendens uni uel
tum dicens. Mulier ecce filius
tuus. deinde dicit ad alium. Ec

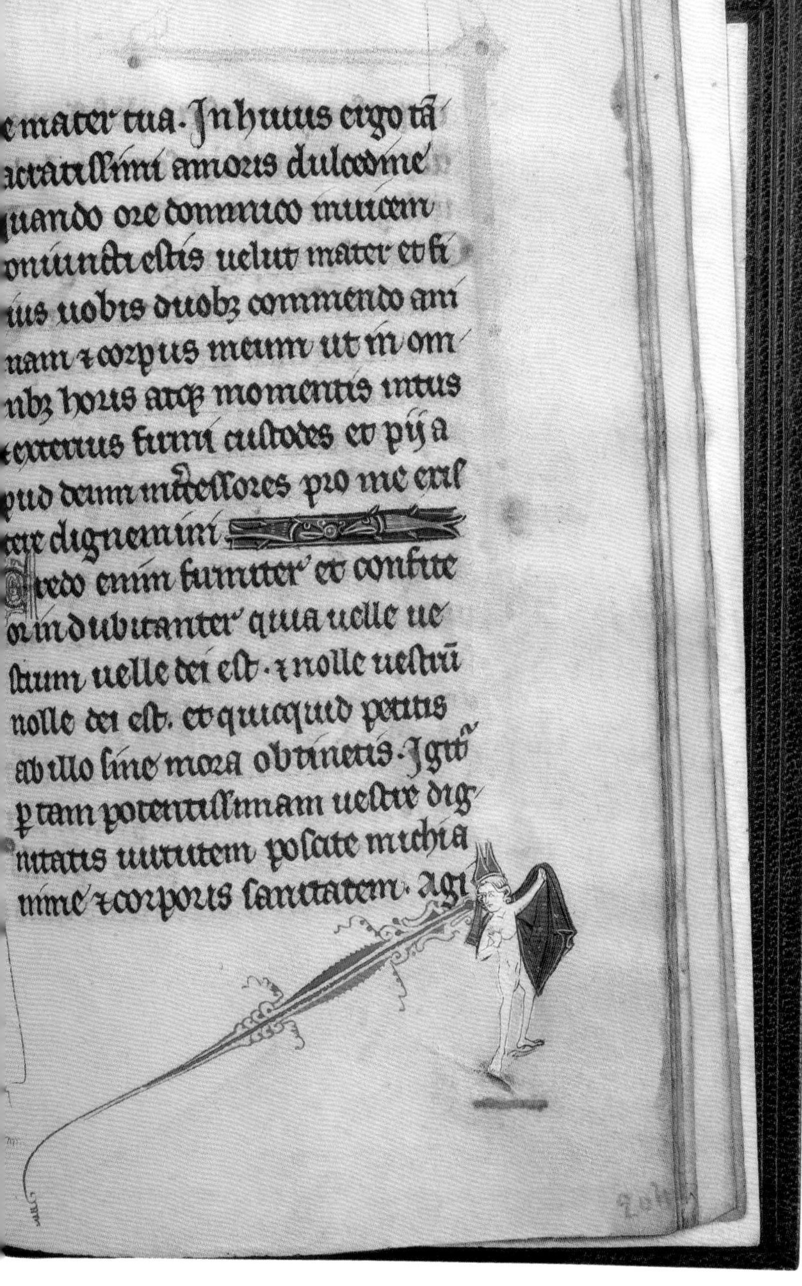

Folios 203v-204r, a woman with a falcon; a bishop unclothing himself

77v, 93v and others), a king (3v), an ape in a king's crown (63r), a seated woman spinning with a distaff (59r), knights in armor (8v and 91r), monks (11r, 45r and 78v), a priest (65v), children (59v, 60r, 79v and others), peasants in hoods (1r, 6v, 64r and others), man in a blue tunic (2r, 3v – with a praying monk – 19r), men with swords (1v, 9v, 37r, 58r – with a scimitar and perhaps therefore a Saracen – 99r, and others), a man with a club (10v, and many others), in one (76r) the club may be a bat and the accompanying dog appears to be guarding balls; a man with a bat hitting something into the air (167r), a boy in blue trousers with a dog (12v), bell-ringers (65r, 73v, 79r and 193r), a viol player (76v), travelers with staffs and shoulder bags (57v and 72r), men with axes (11v, 14v, 57r, 68r, 148r, 200v and others), men with club and drums (2v and 37v), a man with a hammer and a shield (64v), a naked boy with a flail (79v), a man with a hare (11v), archers shooting birds (10v, 13v and 151r), an archer shooting a hare chased by a hound (42v) and shooting a hare (119r, 156v and 201v), an archer shooting what looks like a pie vendor (75r), a man clasping his brow as he stares at a bird (7r), a hunter aiming his sling at a hare (205v), two men blowing trumpets as a hound chases a hare (12r), a man with a club and shield watching a hound and a hare (14r), a bishop blessing (3r and 63v), a jester offering some trick to a grotesque in a cardinal's hat (62v), a bell-ringer standing on his head with a hare on his bottom (203r), naked men (29r, 40v, 50r, 50v, 53r, 55v – protecting his modesty with a gold ball – 86r, 106v, 190r, and others), a naked man with a scimitar and a severed head (185r), grotesques with haloes, crowns, dressed as jesters, battling, and numerous other activities, countless hounds and hares, birds, dragons and other creatures, a blue dog standing upright on a trapeze (67v), a dancing goat (70v), a cat with a man's head (105r and 109r), many women, standing, waving, grasping the penwork, a woman drinking from a bottle (8v), a woman holding out a ring to a knight (66v-67r), a bare-footed girl dancing (5r), a dancing girl with castanets (8r) and other musical instruments (10r and 77r), dancing (61r), a woman in prayer (60v), a girl with a hare (13r), a woman with a falcon (203v), a woman looking into a mirror (204v), mermaids (22v, 27r, 32v, 35v, 36v, 39v, 79v, 86v, 87r, 91v, 92r, and many others), foxes running off with chickens in their mouths (11v and 14v), a grotesque knight fighting a snail (114r), a bird with a gold ring in its beak (22r), a man spearing a lion (3v), a man with an axe chasing a long-tailed hare into a bush while an archer shoots it with an arrow (6r), a man grasping the penwork, watched by a long-tailed hare (6v), hound chasing a hare (1v and very many others), chickens (20v and 21v), peacocks (87v and 124r), a red squirrel (106r), a large pink hound (23v), and many, many others.

PROVENANCE

1. Written for female use for a woman called Marie, who is named in a prayer to God at the top of folio 198v, "famula tua maria" – "your servant Marie;" possibly Marie de Brabant (1256-1321), queen of France, who married Philip III on 21 August 1274 (see above).

2. In Italy by the fifteenth century, when prayers were added on folios 15v-16v and 152r for a man named "Ludovico" or Louis ("indigno famulo tuo Lodovico," folio 16r).

3. It was rebound in Paris by Léon Gruel (1841-1923).

4. Louis-Alexandre Barbet (1850-1931); his sale, Drouot, Paris, 13 June 1932, lot 7.

5. Sold in 1987 by Sam Fogg, London, to the recent owner, who three years later placed it on long-term deposit at the Metropolitan Museum of Art, New York, where it remained until 2017 as MS L.1990.38.

PUBLISHED REFERENCES

A. BENNETT, "A Thirteenth-Century Book of Hours for Marie," *The Journal of the Walters Art Gallery* 54, *Essays in Honor of Lilian M. C. Randall* (1996): 21-50.

B. D. BOEHM, "Recent Acquisitions, A Selection: 1996-1997, Medieval Europe," *The Metropolitan Museum of Art Bulletin* 55, no. 2 (Fall 1997): 21.

J. HIGGITT, *The Murthly Hours: Devotion, Literacy and Luxury in Paris, England and the Gaelic West*, London and Toronto, 2000, p. 182.

K. A. SMITH, *Art, Identity and Devotion in Fourteenth-Century England, Three Women and their Books of Hours*, London and Toronto, 2003, p. 146, n. 99.

A. STONES, "Some Portraits of Women in their Books, Late Thirteenth – Early Fourteenth Century" in A.-M. Legaré, ed., *Livres et Lectures de Femmes en Europe entre Moyen Âge et Renaissance*, Turnhout, 2007, pp. 3-27, at p. 16.

V. REINBURG, "'For the Use of Women': Women and Books of Hours," *Early Modern Women, An Interdisciplinary Journal* 4 (2009): 235-40, at p. 235.

R. A. LESON, "Heraldry and Identity in the Psalter-Hours of Jeanne of Flanders (Manchester, John Rylands Library, Ms. lat. 117)," *Studies in Iconography* 32 (2011): 155-98, at p. 192, n. 52.

A. BENNETT, "Making Literate Lay Women Visible: Text and Image in French and Flemish Books of Hours, 1220-1320," in E. Gertsman and J. Stevenson, eds., *Thresholds of Medieval Visual Culture: Liminal Spaces*, Woodbridge, 2012, pp. 125-58, at pp. xiii, 129, 137 and pls. on pp. 138-42.

S. HINDMAN AND A. BERGERON-FOOTE, *An Intimate Art*, New York, Chicago and Paris, 2012, p. 19 and pl. on p. 32.

A. BENNETT, "Some Perspectives on Two French *Horae* in the Thirteenth Century," in S. Hindman and J. H. Marrow, eds., *Books of Hours Reconsidered*, Turnhout, 2013, pp. 19-40, at p. 25.

A. STONES, *Gothic Manuscripts, 1260-1320*, A Survey of Manuscripts Illuminated in France I, 1, London and Turnhout, 2013-2014, pp. 62, 66 and 118; I, 2, pp. 405 and 494; and II, 2, p. 203 and ills. 345 and 412.

A. SAND, *Vision, Devotion, and Self-Representation in Late Medieval Art*, Cambridge, 2014, p. 339, n. 52.

M. DOYLE, "The Portrait Potential: Gender, Identity and Devotion in Manuscript Owner Portraits, 1230-1320," PhD diss., Bryn Mawr College, 2015, pp. 78 and 175.

R. R. HORDEN COLLERSON, "The Penitential Psalms as a Focus Point for Lay Piety in Late Medieval England," PhD diss., University of Sydney, 2018, pp. 28-29.

FURTHER LITERATURE

ALEXANDRE-BIDON, D. "Prier au féminin? Les livres d'heures des femmes," in A. Cabantous, ed., *Homo Religiosus: Autour de Jean Delumeau*, Paris, 1997, pp. 527-34.

BUETTNER, B. "Women and the Circulation of Books," *Journal of the Early Book Society* 4 (2001): 9-31.

CLANCHY, M. "Did Mothers Teach their Children to Read?," in C. Leyser and L. Smith, eds., *Motherhood, Religion and Society in Medieval Europe, 400-1400, Essays presented to Henrietta Leyser*, Farnham, 2011, pp. 129-53.

DONOVAN, C. *The de Brailes Hours, Shaping the Book of Hours in Thirteenth-Century Oxford*, London, 1991.

GROAG BELL, S. "Medieval Women Book Owners: Arbiters of Lay Piety and Ambassadors of Culture," in M. C. Erler and M. Kowaleski, eds., *Women and Power in the Middle Ages*, Athens (Georgia), 1988, pp. 149-87.

LEGARÉ, A.-M. "Livres d'heures, livres de femmes," *Eulalie* 1 (1998): 53-68.

PENKETH, S. "Women and Books of Hours," in L. Smith and J. H. M. Taylor, eds., *Women and the Book*, London, 1996, pp. 266-81.

Folio 17r, a noblewoman with her daughter kneeling before the Virgin and Child enthroned, an elaborate border including a hunter with hounds chasing a hare, a piebald musician with a viol, a tournament with three galloping knights and two fighting solders judged by a woman with banners and watched by other women on the battlements of a castle

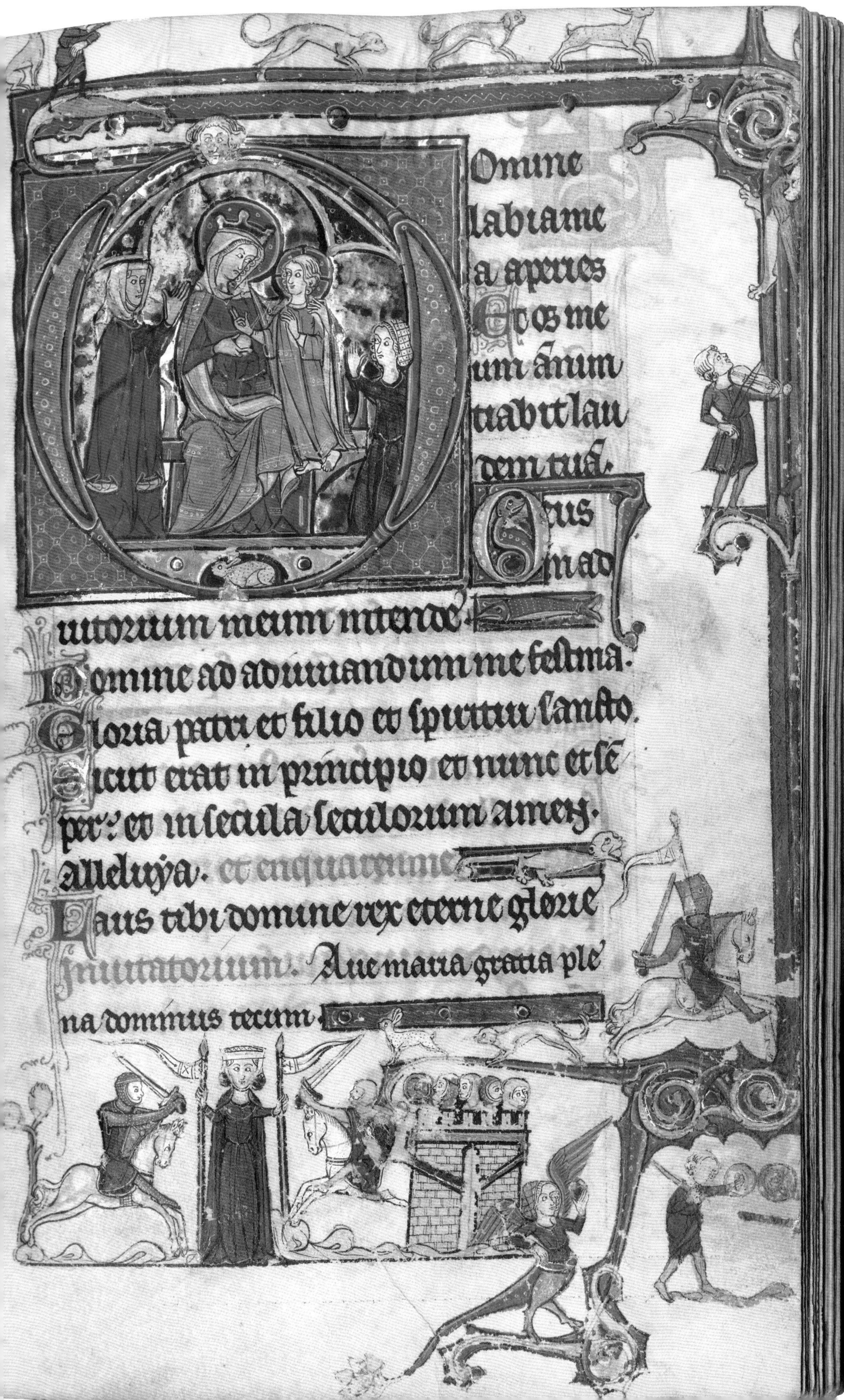

Domine
labia me
a aperies
Et os me
um ānun
ciabit lau
dem tuā.
Deus
in ad
iutorium meum intende.
Domine ad adiuuandum me festina.
Gloria patri et filio et spiritui sancto.
Sicut erat in principio et nunc et sē
per: et in secula seculorum amen.
alleluya. et en quaresme
Laus tibi domine rex eterne glorie
Inuitatorium. Aue maria gratia ple
na dominus tecum

illustrauerat. Et sic ad dī
laudem ⁊ honorem ad edif
ficatōem quoqꝫ ⁊ exēplum
tocius ppli uerone, usqꝫ
in finē uite sue bta uirgo
theuteria perseuerauit.

In finem uero uite sue
in infirmitate corporis
ens. ⁊ susceptis

THE BOOK OF SAINTS THEUTERIA AND TOSCA

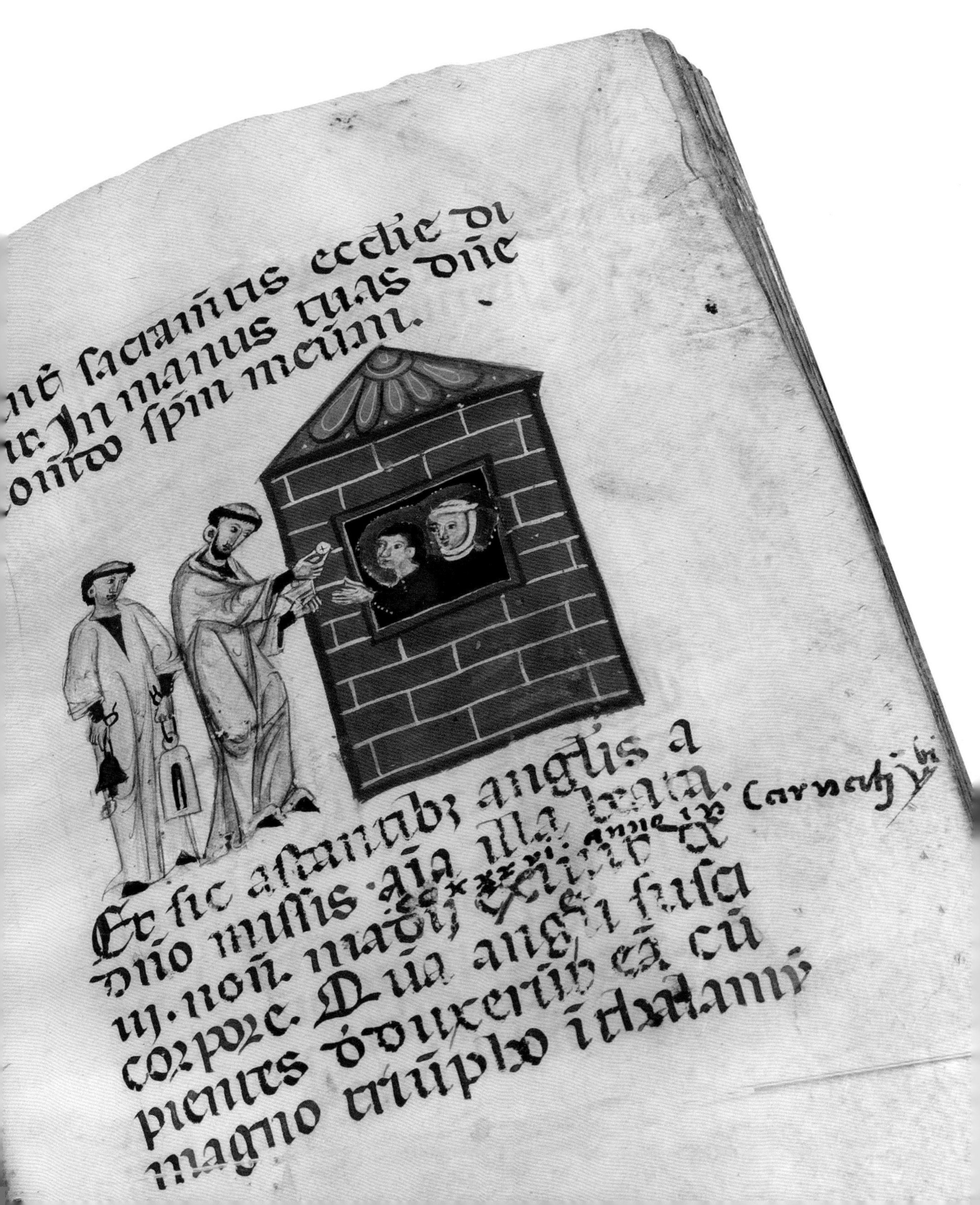

THE BOOK OF SAINTS THEUTERIA AND TOSCA

In Latin, illuminated manuscript on parchment
Italy, Verona, late 13th century
18 miniatures

The unique illuminated medieval manuscript of the lives of two Veronese female saints, one of them English, and the long-lost missing pair to the famous Verona manuscript of the lives of Saints George and Margaret of Antioch (Biblioteca Civica, cod. 1853). Surely made for the tiny Romanesque chapel housing the relics of the saints and most probably written for Bartolomeo della Scala (d. 1304), lord of Verona, and his wife Costanza of Antioch (d. 1301/2), the manuscript was famous in the sixteenth century. Unseen for over four hundred years, it was last described in 1588.

Previous page: Folios 10v-11r, the citizens of Verona praying before the hermitage as Saints Theuteria and Tosca look out of the window; two priests bringing the Last Sacrament to Saint Theuteria, who looks out beside Saint Tosca

Facing page: Folio 1v, Saint Theuteria with her family, two women and three men in noble costume, detail

axuteria: parentib3 gentilib
3 tm̄ nobilibus nata. Q u
diuina gr̄a cooperante: fid
catholice doctrinam ac baptis
gratiam occulte 7 reuerent' suscep
retinuit. Erat namq3 uirgo th
teria decore 7 uenusto aspectu

The little half-underground Romanesque chapel of Sante Theuteria e Tosca is one of the sacred medieval sites of Verona. It is within the complex of buildings around the church of the Santi Apostoli beside the Corso Cavour. There has been a chapel on this site since the fifth century, one of the oldest in the city, but it was rebuilt as a pilgrim shrine with the rediscovery in the twelfth century of the ancient relics of Saints Theuteria and Tosca. The present manuscript was almost certainly intended for use at the shrine itself. It includes two versions of the lives of the saints for public reading, recitations of miracles they performed in Verona, and the texts of the liturgies to be recited in the church, including prayers for the translation of their relics. All these are unique and unpublished. The manuscript, famous in the sixteenth century, has not been seen since 1576.

Civitas Veronensis Depicta, Scipione Maffei, *Verona illustrata*, 1732, copy from Ratherius, c. 10th century, with white circle indicating the location of the Chapel of Saints Theuteria and Tosca (Verona, Biblioteca Capitolare, cod. CXIV (106) fol. 190r, detail)

Folio 1r, King Osgualdus enthroned, speaking to three courtiers

Incipit ystoria vite et transitu beate theuthberie virginis

Legitur in ystoriis anglorum quod cum populus anglie et maxima pars urbium in cinctarum robure ingenuitatis errore eciam apostasia persisteret. vir quidam nomine osgualdus nobilitatis et probitatis pollens. anglicum adeptus est regnum. Et tunc in illis partibus erat quedam puella virgo nomine

est sancte marie magdalene de campo
marcio de verona

In qua quidem ciuitate non
longe ext̄ muros antiquos
dicte ciuitatis inloco quasi
ōsto habitabat inquadam cel
lula mulier quedam religio
sa ⁊ timens deum noīe tu
sca. Que ut dicit̄ soror beati
prodocimi epi. qui tūc tem
epalem uerone regebat. Hec

Folios 3v-4r, the city of Verona, with a church and city gate, and Saint Tosca looking out of the window of her hermitage; Saint Theuteria in conversation with Saint Tosca through the window of the hermitage

bta cherutesa timore pterita
uelocius quam potuit introiuit
Post cuius introitum nutu dei
dicta fenestra statim tellis
araneis est cooperta. ita quod nulla
fractura nullumque uestigium
uidebatur inea.

Et ecce dicti nuntii persequentes
eam per illum locum ostium i
uenerunt dictam cellulam.

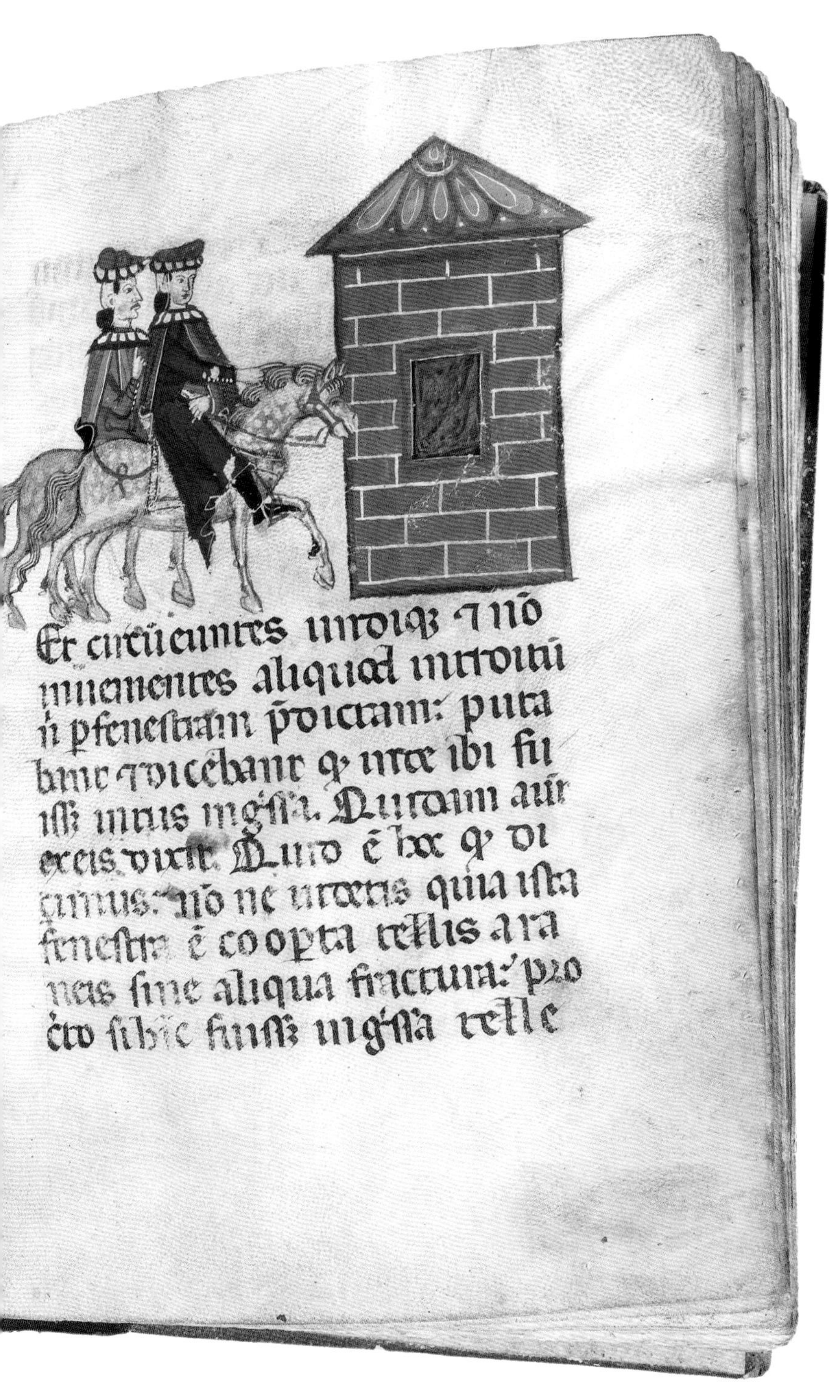

Folios 5v-6r, Saint Theuteria miraculously flying into the hermitage through the small window; the envoys of King Osgualdus arriving at the hermitage and finding no way in, the window miraculously covered with spider webs

Exterior view of the Chapel of Saints Theuteria and Tosca, Verona, 5th-7th centuries

Interior view of the Chapel

Even Wikipedia describes the lives of Saints Theuteria and Tosca as "poorly documented." The present text is incomparably the longest and most detailed in existence. It recounts a tale set in England and Verona. Theuteria herself was British. The manuscript begins by explaining that histories of England tell of a time when the country had returned to paganism. The new king there was called Osgualdus. He fell in love with Theuteria, a beautiful girl of noble parentage, but she had already dedicated her life to Christ and she rejected his advances. The king therefore turned against her and her father. At first, Theuteria concealed herself in a fortified tower near her father's house but she became obliged to flee abroad in pursuit of a monastic life. Travelling through the towns of Europe, she heard tell of the noble and famous city of Verona and so she hastened there. There was an anchoress named Tosca living in a cell in a deserted place outside the city walls. She was said to be a sister of Procululus, bishop of Verona. Theuteria came to Tosca's hermitage and talked with her. In the meantime, at the instigation of the Devil, King Osgualdus had sent agents to Italy to seek out Theuteria, who fled back to Tosca appealing for shelter. However, the hermitage had no door and only a tiny window. Miraculously, Theuteria was taken up through the window, and when the king's agents arrived they rode round and round the hermitage, finding no way in and unable to see her, the small window having been immediately obscured by spider webs. Theuteria implored Tosca to let her stay there. Together they prayed that Osgualdus would be converted to Christianity, and God answered their prayer. Osgualdus was baptized and ordered all the English to become Christian too. One Easter when the king was at lunch with the bishop of his city, the man whose duty it was to give alms to the poor showed the hungry supplicants to the king, who was so moved at their plight that he made them the bearers of his cross, and in his next battle against the pagans Osgualdus won a great victory. Finally, the king died in a place the English call Maserdet on 9 August in the 38th year of his reign [a later annotator adds that this was 212 A.D.], and many miracles took place after his death.

Back in Verona (the manuscript continues), Theuteria and Tosca became famous throughout the region for their piety, and many people visited their hermitage. Eventually Theuteria died, after receiving the Sacrament, on 5 March [236 A.D., according to the annotator] and angels took her to heaven in glory where she was united with her bridegroom Christ, while her body was reverently buried by the faithful and performed many miracles. Sometime later Tosca died too, on 11 July [241 A.D., according to the annotator], and she was laid to rest beside Theuteria, and many miracles were wrought by God at their shrine. In one of these, in the time of the Roman emperor Ycerinus, a certain man was due to be imprisoned for debt in the castle at Villefranche but he prayed to Saint Theuteria who appeared to him dressed in white and all his debts were paid. In another, a woman came with her daughter who was disfigured with a horrible cancer on her face and, with the permission of the priest of the church, they applied the saint's relics and the girl was cured.

cēent fracte. Vn̄ argumentum
ē q̄ nec hic nec aliunde s; int
pōr eē ingressa. Et sic uolunta
te diuina ꝯlusi nō inuenien
tes eam reu̾si sūt ad ꝓpria.

Transacta aūt aliquantula
hora: cognoscentes b̄ta Vbertina
na diuinū auxiliū sibi in tā
ta tribulatione adfuisse in

In a further narrative from folio 20r the story of King Osgualdus is repeated with other details, such as (for example) that his predecessor had been a Christian king called Eadgninus, but that Osgualdus, son of Aicha, sister of Eadgninus, had led Britain back into apostasy when he fell in love with Theuteria.

If there is any transmitted truth in the story, it tells of figures not otherwise known. Osgualdus and Eadgninus are doubtless variants of Oswald and Edwin, and their names echo the family of Oswald, king of Northumbria 634-642, who was indeed a son of Acha, sister of Edwin of Northumbria, king 616-c.632. He died at Maserfield, which may be an acceptable variant of Maserdet, given here. However, Tosca is described as a sister of Saint Procululus, bishop of Verona, who must be Proculus, the bishop who died c. 320. A Roman emperor Ycerinus is not obviously identifiable. Even if the story is fiction (although probably not consciously so), it has its place in the history of creative literature in Italy in the age of Dante, and in the position of women in medieval society. It merits full analysis and publication.

Saint George declares his faith in Christ in front of Diocletian's court, *Passio Sancti Georgii, Passio Sanctæ Margaretæ*, late 13th century (Verona, Biblioteca Civica, cod. 1853, fol. 3v, detail, facsimile edition, 2004)

The name Tosca, for the Veronese heroine of the play by Sardou which became an opera by Puccini, was taken from the saint here.

The manuscript is a hitherto unknown pair to Verona, Biblioteca Civica, cod. 1853, one of the most celebrated Italian illustrated manuscripts of the late thirteenth century. It is written by the same scribe and is illuminated by the same artist. The Verona manuscript comprises the lives of Saint George and Saint Margaret of Antioch, with a slightly later added text in Italian verse in praise of the Virgin Mary. Both books were undoubtedly

Folio 6v, Saint Theuteria inside the hermitage beseeching Saint Tosca to be allowed to remain there, detail

cepit. Et postea ad tantam de
uenit pfectionē. q factus fuit
pimus uexillifer crucis ī illis
Et in pima pugna quā fecit
cō paganos tenens crucem ī
manibz. pimo amonuit pplm
suū dicens.

Flectamus oms genua dnm
oipotentē deprecemur. ut nos

made for the same patron, and the suggestion that this was Bartolomeo della Scala with his wife Costanza of Antioch is consistent with the choice of Greek saints and the courtly iconography echoing the painting of icons and Greek saints' lives from Sicily. The books were both given to the convent of Santa Maria delle Vergine in Campo Marzio, quite possibly by the abbess Alboina della Scala (1311-1375), which was probably when the text in praise of the Virgin Mary was added to the volume in Verona.

Frescoes, Sacristy of the church of the Santi Apostoli, Verona, c. 12th-13th centuries

The manuscripts were undoubtedly illuminated in Verona itself. The uniquely Veronese text of the present volume is confirmation of this. The style can be compared with that of a thirteenth-century illustrated New Testament now in Venice, Collezione Giustiniani cod. 465, which is attributed to the workshops of the cathedral of Verona cathedral (Zanichelli, "Santi e immagini: il manoscritto 1853 della Biblioteca Civica di Verona," pp. 19-82 in D. Bini, cur., *Preghiera alla Vergine con le leggende di San Giorgio e Santa Margherita*, commentary to the facsimile, Modena, 2007). Parallels can be made with frescoes in Verona, in the sacristy of the church of Santi Apostoli, nearby the chapel of the Saint Theuteria and Tosca (E. Arslan, *La pittura e la scultura veronese dal secolo VIII al secolo XIII*, Milan, 1943, p. 172), as well as the previously-Benedictine Monastery of via Provolo (Pietropoli 2004, pp. 183-211). However, the unusually close integration of text and miniatures clearly reflects the fashionable new style of French secular romances then reaching the courts of northeastern Italy, such as that of the La Scala family (Mariani Canova 2005, p. 161).

Folio 8v, King Osgualdus seated at table between his bishop and his almoner, with four poor people in the foreground asking for food, and, to the right, King Osgualdus giving a banner with a crusaders' cross to the four former paupers

illustrauerat. Et sic ad dei
laudem et honorem ad edif
ficationem quoque et exemplum
tocius populi uerone, usque
in finem uite sue beata uirgo
theuteria perseuerauit.

In finem uero uite sue
in infirmitate corporis
laborans. et susceptis reue

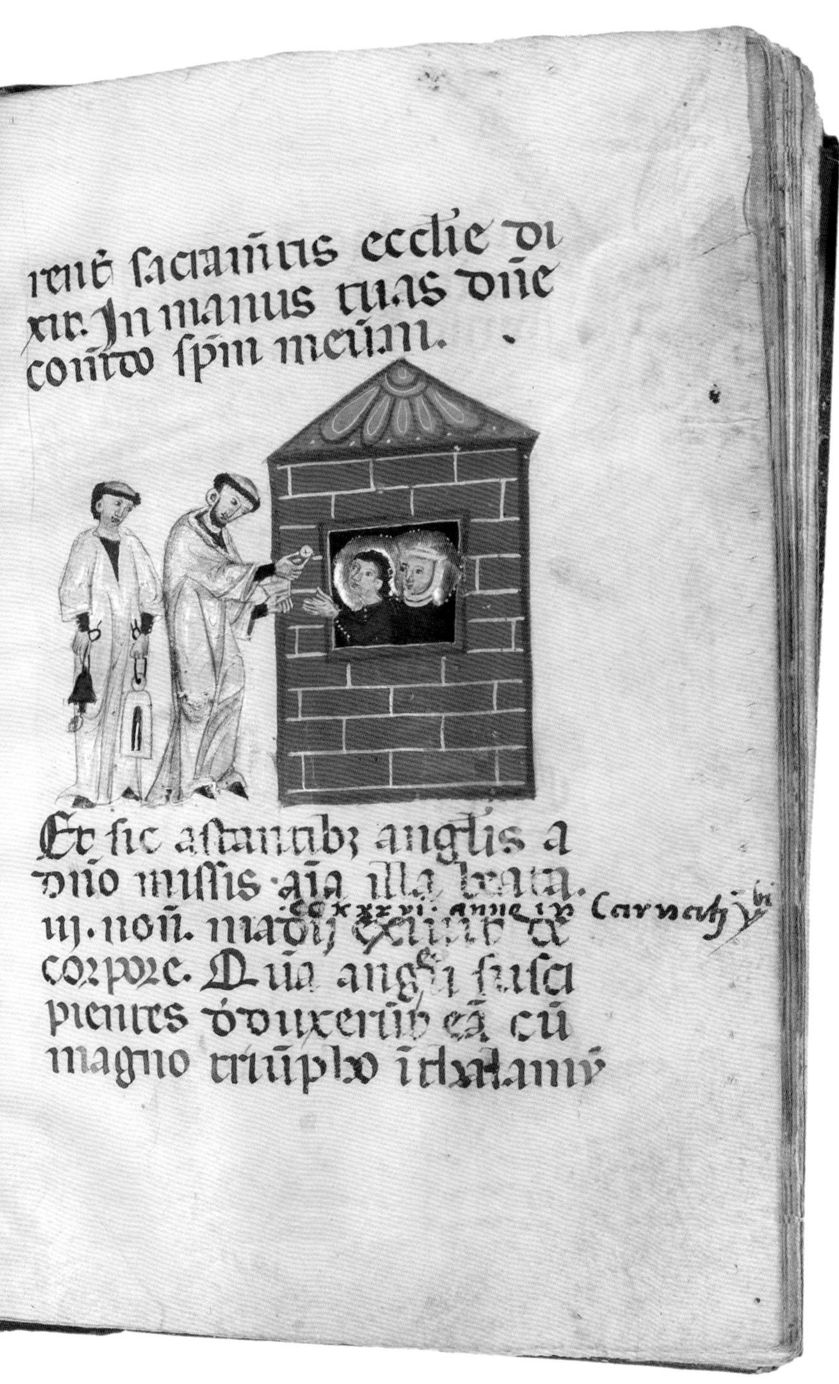

Folios 10v-11r, the citizens of Verona praying before the hermitage as Saints Theuteria and Tosca look out of the window; two priests bringing the Last Sacrament to Saint Theuteria, who looks out beside Saint Tosca

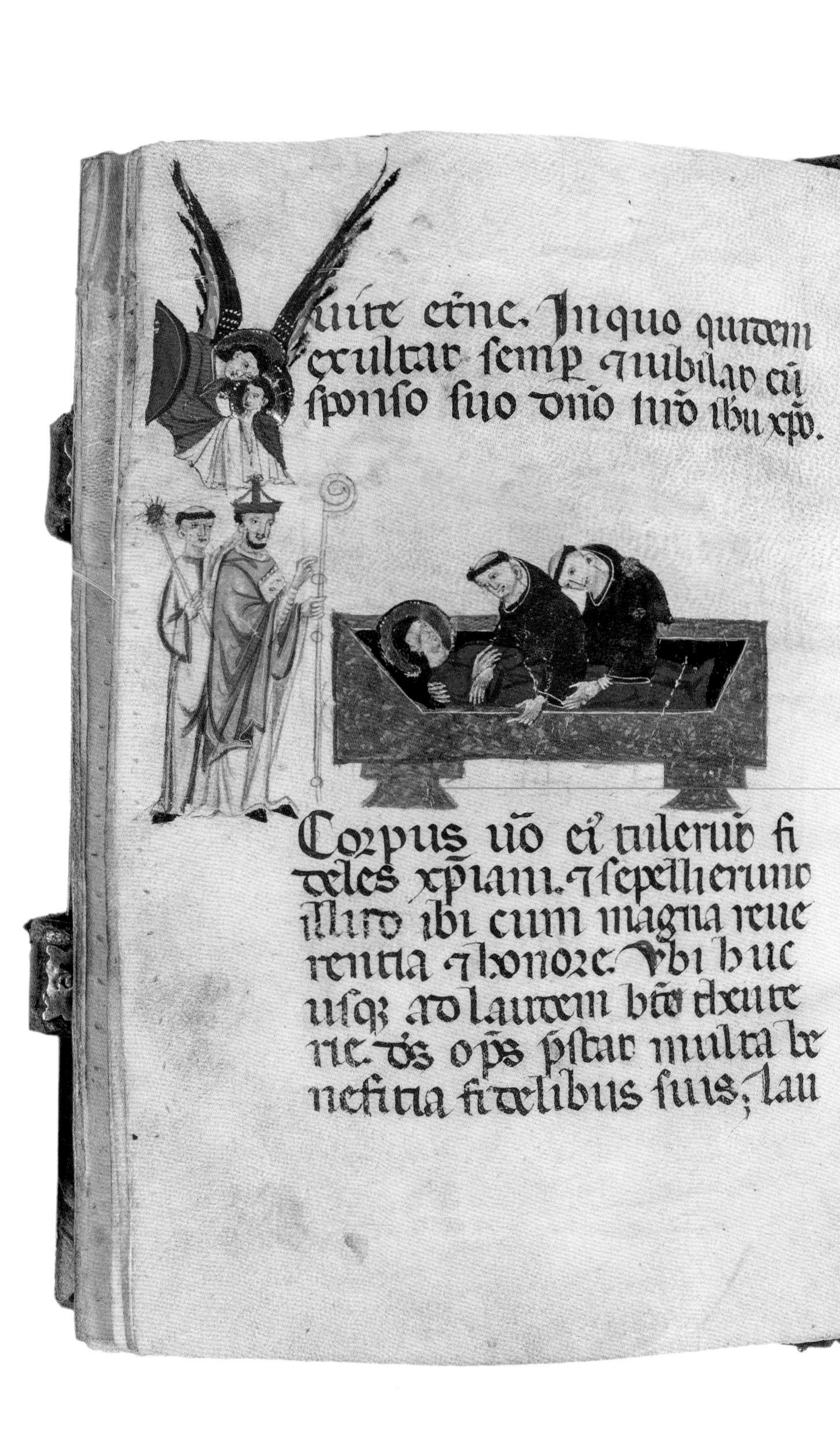

[V]uite eterne. In quo quidem
exultat semp̄ et iubilat cū
sponso suo dn̄o nr̄o ihū xp̄o.

Corpus u°o ei᷒ tulerunt fi
deles xp̄iani. et sepellierunt
illud ibi cum magna reue
rentia et honore. Vbi huc
usq; ad laudem b̄te ckeute
ne. d̄s op̄s p̄stat multa be
neficia fidelibus suis, lau

These are miniatures of enormous charm and a strong and graphic sense of narrative. The narrative continuity is also insured by the depiction of the characters, always wearing the same clothes and ornaments. As in its twin in Verona (Biblioteca Civica cod. 1853), most of the illustrations are inserted without frames in blank space between the text or in the margins. The scene on folio 6v set in the black darkness of the cell is extraordinary. Like a secular romance, it is filled with images of kings and knights and castles. This is a unique manuscript: there was probably no exemplar. Most medieval art is copied from earlier models but, just occasionally, as here, the artist created scenes which were entirely without precedent, and we can glimpse iconography at its moment of invention. Many of the buildings shown would have been known to the artist. Verona cod. 1853 has been reproduced in facsimile (2007). The present manuscript is infinitely worthy of similar publication, and, unlike its pair, it illustrates a tale actually set in Verona itself.

Folio 11v, Saint Theuteria being lifted by an angel to Heaven as two friars lay her body in a sarcophagus blessed by a bishop and a priest

PHYSICAL DESCRIPTION

2 parchment flyleaves + 40 folios on parchment (last 3 originally blank), complete, collation: i-v8, with horizontal catchwords; ruled in faint plummet, single column, folios 1-16r, 19 lines (justification 117 x 76 mm.), folios 16v-19v, 17-18 lines (justification 113 x 76 mm.), folios 20r-36v, 13-16 lines (justification 105 x 76mm.), written in dark brown ink in a relatively large rounded *littera textualis*, some headings in red, capitals touched in red, a few red or blue initials with penwork in the contrasting color, spaces left for a few lines of music never added on folios 18v-19v; 18 illuminated miniatures mostly full-width and about half-page in height in colors and burnished gold, all but the first unframed; inscriptions added at ends, some rubbing and occasional stains, folios 1r and 2v-3r with a few letters of text re-inked where abraded, other small signs of use, generally in good state throughout; contemporary binding of square-edged wooden boards flush with the edges of the pages sewn on 3 thongs, covered with bright red-stained leather, 2 clasps (straps possibly later) from edge of upper cover ending in hinged metal finials fitting over pins on lower cover, parchment pastedowns, binding scuffed and slightly wormed, old leather rebacking, eighteenth-century paper spine title "*di Santa Teuteria Vergine M.SS.*" Dimensions 177 x 120 mm.

The Book of Saints Theuteria and Tosca, binding

TEXT

The manuscript comprises:
Folio 1r, "*Incipit ystoria de vita & transitu beate theutherie virginis*, [L]egitur in ystoriis anglorum ...," ending on folio 15r, "... benedictus in secula seculorum, Amen," followed by miracle stories "His itaque per actis cottidie ...," (folio 15r) "Tempore dominationis impiissimi ycerini ..." (folio 15v) and "Item secundum quod dicitur veronenses ..."
(folio 17r), ending on folio 18r, "... ecclesiam beate th[euterie] de hoc testimonium prohibuit."
Folio 18v, "*ymnum in laudibus*, Laudemus omnes dominum ac beatam theutheriam de cuius sacro corpore verona decorata est ...," ending on folio 20v, "... per infinita secula, amen."
Folio 21r, "*Incipit quedam compilatio de ystoria beati osgualdi & beate theu[terie]*, Legitur enim in tobia, secretum regis cellare bonum est ...," ending on folio 36v, "... dilecte reliquie remanerent."
Folio 36v, "*Oratio, In festo beate theutherie*, Intercessionibus beate theutherie virginis quesumus ...," "Accipe munera quesumus ..." (folio 37r), "*In transactione sive in inventione beate theutherie & tu[sce]*, Omnipotens sempiterne deus qui es virginitatis ..." (folio 37r), ending on folio 37v, "... ad gaudia eterna pertingere per [christum dominum nostrum, Amen]."

ILLUMINATION

The miniatures are:

1. Folio 1r, King Osgualdus enthroned, speaking to three courtiers, within a frame, 60 x 60 mm.

2. Folio 1v, Saint Theuteria with her family, two woman and three men in noble costume, 10 lines (58 mm.) x 64 mm.

3. Folio 3r, Saint Theuteria at home with her mother, indicating the castle where she hoped for safety, 10 lines (75 mm.) x 100 mm.

4. Folio 3v, The city of Verona, with a church and city gate, and Saint Tosca looking out of the window of her hermitage, 10 lines (80 mm.) x 96 mm.

5. Folio 4r, Saint Theuteria in conversation with Saint Tosca through the window of the hermitage, 9 lines (49 mm.) x 54 mm.

6. Folio 4v, King Osgualdus enthroned with his court, sending his envoys in pursuit of Theuteria, 11 lines (66 mm.) x 68 mm.

7. Folio 5r, The envoys riding to Verona, turning their heads back and forth in search of the girl, 9 lines (55 mm.) x 65 mm.

8. Folio 5v, Saint Theuteria miraculously flying into the hermitage through the small window, 9 lines (60 mm.) x 61 mm.

9. Folio 6r, The envoys of King Osgualdus arriving at the hermitage and finding no way in, the window miraculously covered with spider webs, 9 lines (63 mm.) x 92 mm.

10. Folio 6v, Saint Theuteria inside the hermitage beseeching Saint Tosca to be allowed to remain there, 10 lines (58 mm.) x 63 mm.

11. Folio 8v, King Osgualdus seated at table between his bishop and his almoner, with four poor people in the foreground asking for food, and, to the right, King Osgualdus giving a banner with a crusaders' cross to the four former paupers, 10 lines (63 mm.) x 108 mm.

12. Folio 9v, The death of King Osgualdus, lying in bed attended by a bishop, a priest and two family members, 9 lines (50 mm.) x 108 mm.

13. Folio 10v, The citizens of Verona praying before the hermitage as Saints Theuteria and Tosca look out of the window, 11 lines (61 mm.) x 88 mm.

14. Folio 11r, Two priests bringing the Last Sacrament to Saint Theuteria, who looks out beside Saint Tosca, 10 lines (60 mm.) x 68 mm.

15. Folio 11v, Saint Theuteria being lifted by an angel to Heaven as two friars lay her body in a sarcophagus blessed by a bishop and a priest, 9 lines (98 mm. including margin) x 94 mm.

16. Folio 13r, Two priests bringing the Last Sacrament to Saint Tosca, who prays through the window of the hermitage, 9 lines (60 mm.) x 64 mm.

17. Folio 14r, The death of Saint Tosca, lying on a bed beside two candles, attended by a bishop and a deacon, 7 lines (50 mm.) x 83 mm.

18. Folio 14v, The burial of Saint Tosca, whose body is placed in a marble sarcophagus by three friars, attended by a deacon with a cross and a bishop with a book, 9 lines (60 mm.) x 86 mm.

diuina inspiratione mediante
inuenerunt ea nimio odore con
spersa. Tunc deuoti et religiosi
uiri tulerunt ea et posuerunt
in dicta archa cum magna reue
rentia et honore. iiij. nonas
iulij. anno domini m.c.lx. et

Tunc populo cum deuotione a
stante oblationes ac munera
offerentes. clerus sollempniter

diuina celebrauit offitia. Qui
bus reuerent(er) expletis. unu(s)
quisq(ue) remeauit ad p(ro)p(ri)a. cu(m)
laude (et) honore d(omi)ni n(ost)ri ih(es)u
(christi). qui e(st) benedictus in secula
seculorum. Amen.
His itaq(ue) p(er)actis cotidie
excurrebat p(o)p(u)l(u)s ad dict(am)
ecclesiam. (et) cum uenera
tione uisitabat ea(m). Vn(de) inole
uit consuetudo. ut adueni
ente die festiuitatis beate
Toscie. deuote mulieres
ad dicta(m) ecclesiam uenientes in
oratione (et) deuotione p(er)noctaba(n)t.
Ex qua uenerabili (con)suetudi
ne (et) alijs hui(us)modi ueneratio(n)i
omnib(us). multi (et) multe meritis
b(ea)te Toscie diuina iam

Folios 14v-15r, the burial of Saint Tosca, whose body is placed in a marble sarcophagus by three friars, attended by a deacon with a cross and a bishop with a book

PROVENANCE

1. Possibly written for Bartolomeo della Scala (d. 1304), lord of Verona, and his wife Costanza of Antioch (d. 1301/2), daughter of Conrad of Antioch, of the Staufer dynasty of Sicily (see above). He was the first of the Italian rulers to offer refuge to Dante after his expulsion from Florence in 1303 (*Paradiso*, XVII: 70-75). It was presumably intended for the shrine of Sante Teuteria e Tosca attached to the church of the Santi Apostoli in Verona.

2. Given with its companion volume to the Franciscan convent of Santa Maria Maddalene in Campo Marzio in Verona, with their inscription on folio 1r, erased and re-written, "Est sancta marie magdalene de campo martio de Verona." This had originally been a nunnery founded in 1081 as Santa Maria delle Vergine in Campo Marzio, and it had become Franciscan in c. 1226. In 1350 its neighboring house of Santa Maria Maddalene was suppressed and merged with Santa Maria delle Vergine, after which the reconstituted double complex of monastic buildings was popularly known as the "Maddalene." A partially erased inscription probably of the seventeenth century on the flyleaf apparently reads, "Sancta Maria Delle Vergine de ... Maddalene." In the early fourteenth century, the house had been under the patronage of the della Scala family, and several of its members became nuns there, including Bartolomeo's niece Alboina della Scala (1311-1375), abbess from 1332; see G. Sandri, "Scaligere francescane in S. Maria della Vergine di Campomarzo a Verona," in G. Sancassani, ed., *Scritti di Gino Sandri*, Verona, 1969, pp. 135-54, esp. pp.141-47.

The present manuscript together with its sister volume of the lives of Saints George and Margaret of Antioch are very probably the "duo libri a legendis sanctorum" listed in the convent's inventory of 1341 (cf. T. Franco, "Fuori dal mundo: le Clarisse di Santa Maria delle Vergine in Campo Marzio (xiii-xiv secolo)," in V. Terraroli, ed., *Santa Marta Dalla Provianda al Campus universitatario*, Verona, 2015, pp. 15-24, esp. pp. 22-3); Sandri, as above, p. 148.

In 1554 a record of a miracle ascribed to Saint Theuteria was added on folio 38r-v, attesting to her participation in the recovery of "sor lodovico ville, sore de le Magdalene," who had been inflicted for five years with a melancholy which no doctor had been able to cure; her miraculous recovery is witnessed here with an autograph subscription, "io Pietro beroldo physico de le comuni scrissi in Verona." Beroldo is well known as a doctor and philosopher

and founding member of the Veronese Filarmonica (G. Dalle Corte, *L'Istoria di Verona*, 1592, II, p. 716).

The manuscript was seen and described in the convent of Santa Maria Maddalena by Battista Peretti (1522-1611), historian of Verona, who had a transcription made of it, "quale si ritrova nel Monasterio delle venete monache di Campo Marzio di Verona" (*Archivio Veneto*, VIII, i, 1874, p. 168). Its text was the source for the account of Saint Theuteria given in R. Bagata and B. Peretti, *SS. Episcoporum Veronensium Antiqua Monumenta et aliorum sanctorum*, Verona, 1576, folios 70v-71r. Peretti described the manuscript itself in his *Historia delle sante vergini Teuteria et Tosca, con Catalogo de' vesovi di Verona*, Verona, 1588, pp. 28-30, mentioning the miracle attested by Beraldo "in uno libro antico coperto di rosso di carta pecora, nel quale è descritta in Latino l'historia di queste sante" (p. 30). From here the manuscript is reported in the *Acta Sanctorum* for 5 May, XIV, 1680, p. 48, describing it as a "liber rubro operculo..." and "in libro pergameno antique."

Peretti's transcription of the present manuscript on paper, together with notes by him, accompanied by a second manuscript with a translation of the text into Italian, also on paper, both belonged successively to the Veronese antiquarians Giovanni Saibante and the Marchese Paolino de' Gianfilippi (see G. B. Guiliàri, "Sopra alquanti Codici della Libereria Saibante in Verona che escularono dall' Italia," *Archivio Veneto* VIII, i (1874): 143-87, at p. 168, nos. 385-86). They were subsequently sold in the Gianfilippi sale, Paris, 23 January 1843, lot 420 among manuscripts in Hebrew, Greek, and Latin and lot 148 among manuscripts in Italian. They were bought to Gugielmo Libri, sold in 1847 to Lord Ashburnham, and were then part of the negotiated settlement of Libri's Italian manuscripts in 1884 to the Biblioteca Laurenziana in Florence, where they are now Codd. Ashb. 285 and Ashb. 398. As far as we are aware, no other manuscripts of the text have ever existed.

3. The small library of the convent in the Campo Marzio was scattered in the late eighteenth century. The manuscript has a sale price on the upper cover "Zecchini cinque" (5 sequins), the gold currency of the Veneto until 1797. The manuscript's companion volume with the lives of Saints George and Margaret of Antioch was bought locally by the Biblioteca Civica in Verona in 1881. The present manuscript was acquired by the palace library of the marchese Dionisi in Verona, where it has remained until recently.

PUBLISHED REFERENCES

R. BAGATA AND B. PERETTI, *SS. Episcoporum Veronensium Antiqua Monumenta et aliorum sanctorum*, Verona, 1576, folios 70v-71r (the source for the account of Saint Theuteria).

B. PERETTI, *Historia delle sante vergini Teuteria et Tosca, con Catalogo de' vesovi di Verona*, Verona, 1588, pp. 28-30 (description of the manuscript).

FURTHER LITERATURE

The manuscript has not been seen or studied by any scholar since Battista Peretti in the sixteenth century. Its companion volume, Verona, Biblioteca Civica, cod. 1853, is extremely well-published.

For cod. 1853, see the facsimile, *Preghiera alla Vergine. Passio Sancti Georgii. Passio Sanctae Margaretae: Verona, Biblioteca Civica, ms. 1853*, Modena and Milan, 2004, and the commentary volume edited by **A. CONTÒ AND G.Z. ZANICHELLI**, Modena, 2007, including **A. CONTÒ**, "Scheda codicologica del manoscritto 1853 della Biblioteca Civica di Verona," pp. 6-18; **AND G. Z. ZANICHELLI**, "Santi e immagini: il manoscritto 1853 della Biblioteca Civica di Verona," pp. 19-82.

See also:

MARIANI CANOVA, G. "La Miniatura del Duecento in Veneto," in A. Putaturo Murano and A. Petriccioli Saggese, eds., *La Miniatura in Italia, dal tardoantico al Trecento con riferimenti al Medio Oriente e all'Occidente europeo*, Naples, 2005, pp. 156-63.

PETRELLA, G. "La leggenda di Santa Margherita d'Antochia nel ms. 1853 della Biblioteca Civica di Verona e le recensioni miniate della vita della santa," *Revista di storia della miniatura* VIII (2004): 97-106.

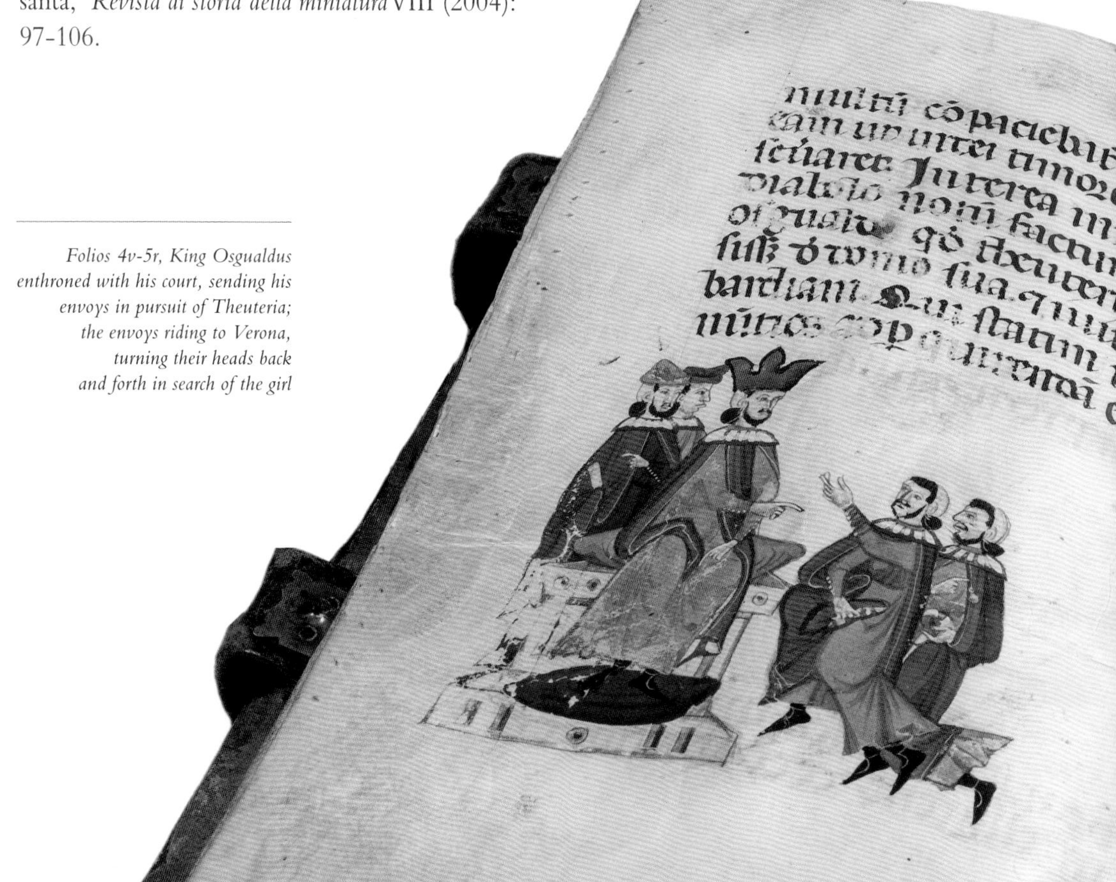

Folios 4v-5r, King Osgualdus enthroned with his court, sending his envoys in pursuit of Theuteria; the envoys riding to Verona, turning their heads back and forth in search of the girl

PIETROPOLI, F. "Verona (VIII-XII secolo)," in F. Flores D'Arcais, ed., *La pittura nel Veneto, Le origini*, Milan, 2004, pp. 153-82.

SESTI, E. "La leggenda di Santa Margherita di Antiochia," in M. Ceccanti and M.C. Castelli, eds., *Il codice miniato. Rapporti tra codice, testo e figurazione, Atti del III congresso di Storia della miniatura (Cortona, 20-23 ottobre 1988)*, Florence, 1992, pp. 363-73.

TONIOLO, F. "La miniatura a Verona al tempo di Ezzelino III," in C. Bertelli and G. Marcadella, eds., *Ezzelini. Signori della Marca nel cuore dell'Impero di Federico II*, exhib., Milan, 2001, pp. 66-69.

TONIOLO, F. "Il Duecento," in G. Castiglioni, ed., *La parola illuminata. Per una storia della miniatura a Verona e Vicenza tra Medioevo e Età Romantica*, Verona, 2011, pp. 13-33.

For the convent of Santa Maria delle Vergine in Campo Marzio (afterwards Santa Maria Maddalene), see:

BIANCOLINI, G.B. *Notizie storiche delle chiese di Verona*, Verona, 1749-71, esp. II, pp. 748-55, III, pp. 70-73, and IV, pp. 717-22.

FRANCO, T. "Fuori dal mondo: le Clarisse di Santa Maria delle Vergini in Campo Marzio (XIII- CIV secolo)," in V. Terraroli, ed., *Santa Marta, Dalla Provianda al Campus universitario*, Verona 2015, pp.15-24.

For the La Scala family and their patronage of art and of the convent of Santa Maria delle Vergine in Campo Marzio, see:

CASTAGNETTI, A. "La famiglia Della Scala sino all'inizio della signoria," in G.M. Varanini, ed., *Gli scaligeri 1277-1387*, exhib., Verona, 1988, pp. 17-18.

CORSO, G. "Il Gran Lombardo e la sua arca," *Bollettino del Comitato Cattolico per l'omaggio a Dante Alighieri* VII (1920), pp. 131-33, and VIII (1921), pp. 16-19.

SANDRI, G. "Scaligere francescane in S. Maria delle Vergini di Campomarzo a Verona," *Le Venezie Francescane* II, no. 3 (1933), reprinted in G. Sancassani, ed., *Scritti di Gino Sandri*, Verona, 1969, pp. 135-54.

We are especially indebted to Gaia Grizzi and Laura Nuvoloni for help with the bibliography.

Nolite confide(re) in principibz: nec in filiis ho
minum in quibz no(n) e(st) salus. Exibit sp(iritu)s eius ⁊
revertetur in t(er)ram suam: in illa die peribunt omnes
cogitationes eorum. Beatus cuius d(eu)s iacob adiu
tor eius spes eius in d(omi)no deo ipsius qui fecit ce
lum ⁊ t(er)ram: mare ⁊ omnia que in eis s(un)t. Qui
custodit veritatem in s(e)c(u)l(u)m: facit iudicium iniu
riam patientibz: dat escam esurientibz. D(omi)n(u)s
solvit compeditos: d(omi)n(u)s illuminat cecos. Do
105 minus erigit elisos: d(omi)n(u)s diligit iustos. D(omi)n(u)s
custodit advenas pupillum ⁊ viduam susci
piet ⁊ vias p(e)cc(at)orum disperdet. Regnabit d(omi)n(u)s in s(e)c(u)la
deus tuus syon: in generatione ⁊ generatione. Al
Laudate d(omi)n(u)m q(uonia)m bonus e(st) psalm(us): luia
deo n(ost)ro sit iocunda decoraq(ue) laudatio.
Edificans ier(usa)l(e)m d(omi)n(u)s: dispersiones isr(ae)l(is) congre
gabit. Qui sanat contritos corde: ⁊ alligat con
tritiones eorum. Qui numerat multitudinem stellarum
⁊ omnibz eis nomina vocans. Magnus d(omi)n(u)s n(oste)r
⁊ magna virtus eius: ⁊ sapientie eius no(n) e(st) nume
rus. Suscipiens mansuetos d(omi)n(u)s: humilians
a(utem) p(ec)c(at)ores usq(ue) ad t(er)ram. Precinite d(omi)no in confes
sione: psallite deo n(ost)ro in cythara. Qui operit celu(m)
nubibz: ⁊ parat t(er)re pluviam. Qui producit in mo(n)
tibz fenu(m): ⁊ herbam servituti hominu(m). Qui dat
iumentis escam ipsorum: ⁊ pullis corvorum invoca(n)
tibz eum. Non in fortitudine equi voluntate(m)
habebit: nec in tibiis viri beneplacitu(m) erit ei. Be
neplacitum e(st) d(omi)no s(upe)r timentes eu(m): ⁊ in eis qui
sperant s(upe)r mi(sericordi)a eius. Al(lelui)a. aggei ⁊ zachar(ie).
Lauda ier(usa)l(e)m d(omi)n(u)m: lauda d(eu)m tuum sy
on. Q(uonia)m confortavit seras portaru(m)
tuar(um): b(e)n(e)dixit filiis tuis in te. Qui posuit fi
nes tuos pacem: ⁊ adipe frumenti saciat te. Qui
emittit eloquiu(m) suu(m) t(er)re: velocit(er) currit sermo
eius. Qui dat nivem sic(ut) lana(m): nebulam sic(ut) ci
nerem spargit. Mittit cristallu(m) suu(m) sic(ut) bu
ccellas: ante facie(m) frigoris eius quis sustinebit.
Emittet verbum suu(m) ⁊ liquefaciet ea: flab(it) sp(iritu)s
[eiu]s ⁊ fluent aque. Qui annunciat verbum
Laudate d(omi)n(u)m de celis: laudate eum in ex
celsis. Laudate eum om(ne)s angeli eius: lau
[date] eum om(ne)s virtutes eius. Laudate eum sol ⁊ lu
na: laudate eum om(ne)s stelle ⁊ lumen. Lau
[dat]e celi celorum: ⁊ aque q(ue) s(upe)r celos sunt lau
[dent nomen] d(omi)ni. Quia ip(s)e dixit ⁊ f(ac)ta s(un)t: ip(s)e ma(n)
[davit ⁊ cre]ata s(un)t. Statuit ea in et(er)nu(m) ⁊ in s(e)c(u)l(u)m
[s(e)c(u)li: precept]u(m) posuit ⁊ no(n) p(re)t(er)ibit. Laudate do
[minum de terra: dr]achones ⁊ om(ne)s abyssi. Ignis

[...]al ⁊ iudicia sua isr(ae)l. Non fe(cit)
[...]iudicia sua n(on) manifestavit eis.

grando nix glacies sp(iritu)s p(ro)cellar(um): qui faciu(n)t ver
bum eius. Montes ⁊ om(ne)s colles: ligna fru(cti)
fera ⁊ om(ne)s cedri. Bestie ⁊ universa pecora: ser(pen)
tes ⁊ volucres pennate. Reges t(er)re ⁊ om(ne)s p(o)p(u)li:
principes ⁊ om(ne)s iudices t(er)re. Iuvenes ⁊ virg(i)
nes senes cum iunioribz laudent nom(en) d(omi)ni: q(ui)a
exaltatum e(st) nom(en) eius solius. Confessio
eius s(upe)r celum ⁊ t(er)ram: ⁊ exaltavit cornu p(o)p(u)li sui.
Hymnus omnibz s(an)c(t)is eius: filiis isr(ae)l p(o)p(u)lo ap
propinquanti sibi. Al(lelui)a.
Cantate domino canticum novu(m): laus
eius in ecc(lesi)a s(an)c(t)orum. Letetur isr(ae)l in eo qui
fecit eum: ⁊ filie syon exultent in rege suo.
Laudent nom(en) eius in choro: in tympano ⁊ psal
terio psallant ei. Quia beneplacitum e(st) d(omi)no in
p(o)p(u)lo suo: ⁊ exaltabit mansuetos in salute(m).
Exul
tabunt s(an)c(t)i in gl(ori)a: letabuntur in cubilibz suis.
Exultationes dei in gutture eor(um): ⁊ glad(ii)
ancipites in manibz eor(um). Ad faciendam vin
dictam in nationibz: increpationes in p(o)p(u)lis.
Ad alligandos reges eor(um) in compedibz: ⁊ nobiles e
or(um) in manicis ferreis. Ut faciant in eis iudi
cium conscriptum: gl(ori)a h(ec) e(st) omnibz s(an)c(t)is ei(us). Al(lelui)a.
Laudate d(omi)n(u)m in s(an)c(t)is eius: laudate eum in
firmamento virtutis eius. Laudate eum in
virtutibz eius: laudate eum s(ecundu)m multitudi
nem magnitudinis eius. Laudate eum in so
no tube: laudate eum in psalterio ⁊ cythara. Lau
date eum in tympano ⁊ choro: laudate eum in
cordis ⁊ organo. Laudate eum in cymbalis be
ne sonantibz: laudate eum in cymbalis iubi 170
lationis: omnis sp(iritu)s laudet d(omi)n(u)m.

THE ROYAL PSALTER GROUP BIBLE

THE ROYAL PSALTER GROUP BIBLE

In Latin, illuminated manuscript on parchment
Northern France, Paris, c. 1270-1280
77 large historiated initials by the Royal Psalter Group

The manuscript here is among the largest one-volume Parisian Bibles imaginable, about 13½ inches in height and massive in weight. It is a thirteenth-century Bible made for astonishing display. Painted by the Royal Psalter Group responsible for the celebrated Psalter of Saint Louis and other manuscripts commissioned by members in the royal circle, this Bible bears the hallmarks of that refined style. It is in breathtaking and impeccable condition with generous margins setting off brilliant and colorful images, both figural and purely ornamental, often with complex architecture – truly a shimmering "pocket Cathedral."

Previous page: Folios 207v-208r, Initial 'I' including three grotesques; King Solomon seated with a birch rod looking down at a diminutive child with a book, doubtless his son Rehoboam, Proverbs
Facing page: Folio 1r, Saint Jerome writing, seated at a desk in a gothic enclosure, general prologue

reduced

prefecit godoliam filium aicham filii saphan
Qd cum audissent omnes duces militum ipsi et
uiri qui erant cum eis uidelicet quod constituisset rex
babil godoliam: uenerunt ad godoliam in
masphat. ysmael filius nathanie et iohanan
filius charee et saraia filius thenameth nero
phatites et iezonias filius machati ipsi et so
cii eorum. Iurauitque eis godolias et sociis eorum di
cens. Nolite timere seruire chaldeis. mane
te in terra et seruite regi babilonis et bene erit uob.
Factum est autem in mense vii. uenit ysmael filius
nathanie filii elysama de semine regio et x. ui
ri cum eo. Percusseruntque godoliam qui et mor
tuus est. Sed et iudeos et chaldeos qui erant cum eo in
masphat. Consurgensque omnis populus a paruo usque
ad magnum et principes militum uenerunt in e
gyptum timentes chaldeos. Factum est autem in anno
xxxvii. transmigrationis ioachim regis iude
mense xii. xxvii. mensis die subleuauit euil
meradach rex babilonis anno quo regnare ce
perat caput ioachim regis iuda de carcere et locutus est
ei benigne et posuit thronum eius super thronum re
gum qui erant cum eo in babilone et mutauit
uestes eius quas habuerat in carcere et comedebat pa
nem semper in conspectu eius cunctis diebus ui
te sue. annona quoque constituit ei sine intermi
ssione que et dabatur ei a rege per singulos dies uite
sue. Incipit prologus in primo libro paralipomenon

Si septuaginta interpretum pu
ra et ut ab eis in grecum uersa est
editio permaneret. superflue me mi
chromati episcoporum sanctissime atque
doctissime impelleres ut tibi
hebrea uolumina latino ser
mone transferrem. Quod enim semel aures hominum
occupauerat et nascentis ecclesie roborauerat fidem iu
stum erat etiam nostro silentio comprobari. Nunc uero cum
pro uarietate regionum diuersa ferantur exempla
ria et germana illa antiquaque translatio cor
rupta sit atque uiolata nostri arbitrii putas aut
e pluribus iudicare quod uerum sit aut nouum opus in
ueteri opere condere illudentibusque iudeis cornicum ut
dicitur oculos configere. Alexandria et egyptus in lxx
suis hesitium laudat auctorem. Constantinopo
lis usque ad antiochiam luciani martiris exempla
ria probat. Medie inter has prouincie
palestinos codices legunt quos ab origene ela
boratos eusebius et pamphilus uulgauerunt.
totusque orbis hac inter se trifaria uarietate com

pugnat. Et certe origenes non solum exem
pla composuit quatuor editionum e regione sin
gula uerba describens ut unus dissentiens sta
tim ceteris inter se consentientibus arguatur. sed
quod maioris audacie est in editione lxx theodoci
onis editionem miscuit asteriscis designans que
minus fuerant et uirgulis que ex superfluo uideban
tur apposita. Si igitur aliis licuit non tenere quod semel
acceperant et post lxx cellulas que uulgo sine aucto
re iactantur singulas cellas aperire. hocque in ec
clesiis legitur quod lxx nescierunt. cur me non
suscipiant latini mei qui inuiolata editione
ueteri ita nouam condidi ut laborem meum
hebreis et quod maius est apostolis auctoribus probem. in
Scripsi nuper librum de optimo genere interpre
tandi. ostendens illa de euangelio. ex egypto
uocaui filium meum et quoniam nazareus uocabi
tur et uidebunt in quem compunxerunt. et illud
apostoli. Quod oculus non uidit. nec auris audiuit. nec in cor
hominis ascendit que preparauit deus diligentibus se. ceteraque his similia in he
breorum libris inueniri. Certe apostoli et euangeliste
lxx interpretes nouerant et unde eis hoc dicere que
in lxx interpretibus non habetur. Christus deus noster utrius
que testamenti conditor in euangelio secundum
iohannem. Qui credit inquit in me sicut dicit scrip
tura. flumina de uentre eius fluent aque
uiue. Utique scriptum est quod saluator scriptum esse
testatur. Ubi scriptum est. lxx non habent. apocripha nes
cit ecclesia. Ad hebreos igitur reuertendum est. unde et
dominus loquitur et discipuli exempla presumunt.
pauca uerum loquor et obtrectatoribus meis tan
respondeo qui canino dente me rodunt in
publico detrahentes. legentes in angulis. iidem
accusatores et defensores. cum in aliis probent
quod in me reprobant quasi uirtus et uitium non in re
bus sit. sed cum auctore mutetur. Ceterum me
mini editionem lxx translatorum olim de greco
emendatam tribuisse me nostris nec inimi
cum debere estimari eorum quos in conuen
tu fratrum semper edissero. Et quod nunc dabreia
min. id est uerba dierum interpretatus sum. idcirco
feci ut inextricabiles moras et siluam
nominum que scriptorum confusa sunt
uitio sensuumque barbariem apertius et per
uersuum cola digererem. michimet ipsi
et meis iuxta hismenium canens surde
sint ceterorum. Incipit primus liber paralipomenon

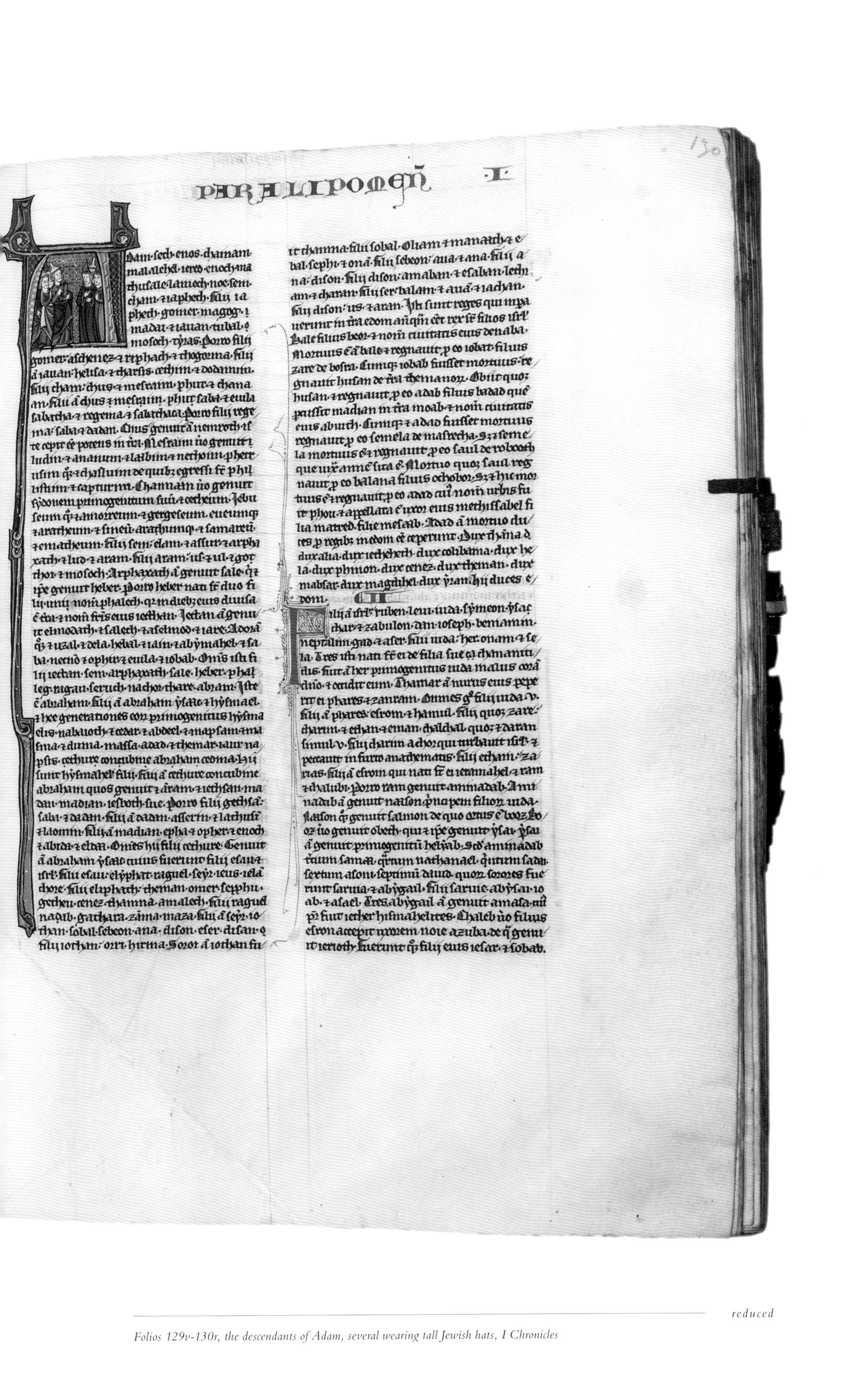

reduced

Folios 129v-130r, the descendants of Adam, several wearing tall Jewish hats, I Chronicles

Probably the two most enduring inventions of the thirteenth century were Gothic architecture and the one-volume Latin Bible. The books of the Old and New Testaments in the Latin translation ascribed principally to Jerome (c. 342-420) were the most fundamental texts of the European Middle Ages, but they had usually been made either as separate components or in huge sets of multiple volumes. The arrangement of all the various texts of the Bible into a standard order and the compression of this entirety of the Scriptures into single portable volumes began to take place in the late twelfth century. A new kind of Bible was perfected in Paris in the first half of the thirteenth century. It is an invention still in use today, for all modern Bibles follow that Parisian order of the texts and the numbering of the chapters, and most still use the thirteenth-century practices of double columns, running-titles along the tops of pages, and dictionaries of names at the end. Most thirteenth-century Bibles were tiny, the size of saddlebags of travelling friars. Just occasionally, luxury versions were made on a vast scale. Usually these were in several volumes, like the Carysfort Bible (Sotheby's, 5 July 2005, lot 48) or the Bible of Cardinal Duprat in the Boston Public Library (J. F. Hamburger et al, eds., *Beyond Words: Illuminated Manuscripts in Boston Collections*, Boston, 2016, p. 110, no. 83). The manuscript here is among the largest one-volume Parisian Bibles imaginable, about 13½ inches in height and massive in weight. It is a thirteenth-century Bible made for astonishing display.

Folio 173r, Queen Vashti standing looking up at King Ahasuerus in the citadel of Susa, Esther

suas. Porro iudith universa arma bellica o-
lofernis que dedit illi populus et canopeum quod ipsa
abstulerat in anathema oblivionis tradidit.
Erat autem populus iocundus secundum faciem sanctorum et per tres
menses huius victorie gaudium celebratum
est cum iudith. Post dies autem illos unusquisque in
rediit in sua et iudith magna facta est in bethulia et preclarior erat universis terre israel. Erat enim virtuti castitas adiuncta ut non cognosceret virum
omnibus diebus vite sue ex quo defunctus est ma-
nasses vir eius. Erat autem festis diebus procedens
cum gloria magna. Mansit autem in domo viri sui
annos centum et quinque et dimisit abram suam liberam et de-
functa est ac sepulta cum viro suo in bethulia et
luxeruntque illam omnis populus diebus septem. In omni autem
spatio vite eius non fuit qui perturbaret israel
et post mortem eius multis annis. Dies autem victorie huius festivitatis ab hebreis in numero
sanctorum dierum accipitur et colitur a iudeis ex illo tempore usque in presentem diem. Incipit prologus

Librum hester variis hester
translatoribus constat esse vitiatum
quem ego de archivis hebreorum rele-
vans verbum e verbo expressius
transtuli. Quem librum editio vulgata lacini-
osis hinc inde verborum funibus trahit addens ea
que ex tempore dici poterant et audiri sicut solu-
tum est scolaribus disciplinis sumptoque themate
excogitare quibus verbis uti potuit qui iniuriam passus est vel ille qui iniuriam fecit. Vos autem
o paula et eustochium quoniam et bibliothecas hebreorum studuistis intrare et interpretum certamina comprobastis tenentes hester hebraicum
librum per singula verba nostram translationem as-
picite ut possitis cognoscere me nihil etiam augmen-
tasse addendo sed fideli testimonio simpliciter
sicut in hebreo habetur historiam hebraicam in
latine lingue tradidisse. Nec affectamus la-
udes hominum nec vituperationes expavescimus.
Deo enim placere curantes minas hominum
penitus non timemus. Quoniam dissipat deus ossa eorum qui hominibus placere desiderant et
secundum apostolum qui eiusmodi sunt servi christi esse
non possunt. Rursum in libro hester alpha-
betum ex minio usque theta litteram fecimus
in diversis locis volentes scilicet hoc interpretum ordinem per hoc insinuare studioso lectori. Nos enim iuxta
morem hebreorum ordinem prosequi in hac editione ma-
luimus. Incipit liber hester

In diebus assueri qui regnavit ab yndia
usque ethiopiam super centum viginti septem provincias quando
sedit in solio regni sui. Susa civitas
regni eius exordium fuit. Tertio igitur anno
imperii sui fecit grande convivium cunctis principibus et pueris suis fortissimis
persarum et medorum inclitis et prefectis provinci-
arum coram se ut ostenderet divitias glorie
regni sui ac magnitudinem atque iactan-
tiam potentie sue multo tempore centum videlicet
et octoginta diebus. Cumque complerentur dies
convivii invitavit omnem populum qui in-
ventus est in susis a maximo usque ad mi-
nimum et diebus septem iussit convivium
preparari in vestibulo orti et nemoris quod
regio cultu et manu consitum erat. Et pen-
debant ex omni parte tentoria coloris aerii
et carpasini ac iacinctini sustentata funibus bissinis ac purpureis qui ebur-
neis circulis inserti erant et columpnis
marmoreis fulciebantur. Lectuli quoque
aurei et argentei super pavimentum sma-
ragdino et pario stratum lapide dis-
positi erant quod mira varietate pictu-
ra decorabat. Bibebant autem qui invita-
ti erant aureis poculis et aliis atque aliis va-
sis cibi inferebantur. Vinum quoque ut magnifi-
centia regia dignum erat habundans et precipu-
um ponebatur. Nec erat qui nolentes cogeret
ad bibendum. Sed sic rex constituerat preponens
mensis singulos de principibus suis ut sume-
ret unusquisque quod vellet. Vasthi quoque regina fecit convivium feminarum in palatio ubi rex
assuerus manere consueverat. Itaque die septimo cum
rex esset hylarior et post nimiam potationem in-
caluisset mero precepit naumam et bazatam et
arbana et bagata et zarath et abgatha et car-
chas septem eunuchis qui in conspectu eius mi-
nistrabant ut adducerent reginam vasthi coram rege posito super caput eius diademate ut ostenderet cunctis populis et principibus illius pul-
chritudinem. Erat enim pulchra valde. Que renu-
it et ad regis imperium quod per eunuchos manda-
verat venire contempsit. Unde iratus rex et
nimio furore succensus interrogavit sapientes qui ex more regio semper ei aderebant et
illorum faciebat cuncta consilio scientium leges
ac iura maiorum. Erant autem primi et proximi carse-
na et sethar et admatha et tharsis et mares et

David and Bathsheba and David in Prayer in an initial 'B,' *Psalter of Saint Louis*, illuminated by the Royal Psalter Group, c. 1260-1270 (Paris, BnF, MS lat. 10525, f. 184)

The illustrations are attributable to the artists of the great Psalter of Saint Louis (Paris, Bibliothèque nationale de France, MS lat. 10525), "justly renowned as one of the most refined in the history of medieval illumination and book-making" (Stones, I, ii, p. 21). The Psalter was illuminated in Paris around 1260-1270 and is illustrated with seventy-eight full-page paintings. It remained in the libraries of the French royal family until 1400, when King Charles VI gave it to his daughter, a nun of Poissy Abbey. The same workshop had earlier illuminated the Psalter and Hours of Isabelle of France, sister of Saint Louis (now Cambridge, Fitzwilliam Museum MS 300), "among the finest achievements of the artists, scribes and patrons who transformed thirteenth-century Paris into the leading European center of manuscript production" (S. Panayotova and P. Binski, eds., *The Cambridge Illuminations*, London, 2005, p. 179).

eam quam plantavit dextera tua: et super filium hominis
confirmasti tibi. Incensa igni et suffossa: ab
increpatione vultus tui peribunt. Fiat ma
nus tua super virum dextere tue: et super filium hominis
quem confirmasti tibi. Et non discedimus a te:
vivificabis nos et nomen tuum invocabimus.
Domine deus virtutum converte nos: et ostende
faciem tuam et salvi erimus.

Exultate deo adiutori nostro:
iubilate deo iacob. Su
mite psalmum et date ty
mpanum: psalterium io
cundum cum cythara.
Buccinate in neomeni
a: in insigni die sollemp
nitatis nostre. Quia pre
ceptum in israel est: et iudicium deo iacob. Testimo
nium in ioseph posuit illud cum exiret de terra
egypti: linguam quam non noverat audivit.
Divertit ab oneribus dorsum eius: manus eius
in cophino servierunt. In tribulatione invo
casti me et liberavi te: exaudivi te in abscondi
to tempestatis: probavi te apud aquam contradic
tionis. Audi populus meus et contestabor te: israel
si audieris me non erit in te deus recens neque ado
rabis deum alienum. Ego enim sum dominus deus tuus
qui eduxi te de terra egypti: dilata os tuum et im
plebo illud. Et non audivit populus meus vocem
meam: et israel non intendit mihi. Et dimisi eos secundum deside
ria cordis eorum: ibunt in adinventionibus suis.
Si populus meus audisset me: israel si in viis meis
ambulasset. Pro nichilo forsitan inimicos
eorum humiliassem et super tribulantes eos misis
sem manum meam. Inimici domini mentiti sunt
ei: et erit tempus eorum in secula. Et cibavit illos
ex adipe frumenti: et de petra melle saturavit
eos.

Deus stetit in synagoga deorum: in medio autem
deos diiudicat. Usquequo iudicatis
iniquitatem: et facies peccatorum sumitis. Iudica
te egeno et pupillo: humilem et pauperem iusti
ficate. Eripite pauperem: et egenum de manu pec
catoris liberate. Nescierunt neque intellexerunt
in tenebris ambulant: movebuntur omnia
fundamenta terre. Ego dixi dii estis: et filii excel
si omnes. Vos autem sicut homines moriemini: et sicut
unus de principibus cadetis. Surge deus iu
dica terram: quoniam tu hereditabis in omnibus gen
tibus.

Deus quis similis erit ti
compescaris deus. Quoniam
sonuerunt: et qui oderunt te ex
Super populum tuum malignaveru
taverunt adversus sanctos tuos. D
te et disperdamus eos de gente: et
men israel ultra. Quoniam cogitave
simul adversum te testamenti
tabernacula ydumeorum et hismael
gareni gebal et amon et amalec
habitantibus tyrum. Etenim as
facti sunt in adiutorium filiis l
sicut madian et sisare: sicut iabin
Disperierunt in endor: facti sunt
Pone principes eorum sicut oreb et z
mana. Omnes principes eorum
hereditate possideamus sanctuari
meus pone illos ut rotam: et sicut st
faciem venti. Sicut ignis qu
vam: et sicut flamma comburens m
sequeris illos in tempestate tua
babis eos. Imple facies eorum
querent nomen tuum domine. Erubesc
tur in seculum seculi: et confundant
cognoscant quia nomen tibi dominus: tu
mus in omni terra.

Quam dilecta tabernacula
tua domine virtutum: concu
anima mea in atria domini. Cor me
ultaverunt in deum vivum. Etenim p
sibi domum: et turtur nidum ubi
suos. Altaria tua domine virtuti
meus. Beati qui habitant in domo
seculorum laudabunt te. Beatus
auxilium abs te: ascensiones in c
suit in valle lacrimarum: in loc
Etenim benedictionem dabit legisl
civitate virtute in virtutem: vid
in syon. Domine deus virtutum
meam: auribus percipe deus iacob. P
pice deus: et respice in faciem christi t
melior est dies una in atriis tuis super m
abiectus esse in domo dei mei: ma
in tabernaculis peccatorum. Quia misericordia
ligit deus: gratiam et gloriam dabit dominus
bit bonis eos qui ambulant in
domine virtutum beatus homo qui

The miniatures in the Bible have all the features of the workshop's style as defined by Branner (1977, p. 135), including elongated feet, rubbery arms as if without bones, tilted heads, teardrop eyes, and spectacular drapery in architectural settings. Hairstyles are identical, often with little rolls of hair along the fringe. Dramatic profiles are a notable feature of the Psalter of Saint Louis. They recur precisely here in figures such as the fool (folio 194r), Solomon (folio 208r), Odadiah (folio 310r), and many others. Faces sometimes have little smiley mouths and pink cheeks. The great broad decorative initial 'I' on folio 208r is filled with scrolling leaves and grotesques exactly like the frames surrounding all miniatures in Saint Louis' Psalter. Architecture is often complex and tall and insubstantial, like the pillars of the Sainte-Chapelle. Colors are vibrant. Comparison of thirteenth-century illumination with stained-glass windows is commonplace, but true. There are whimsical animals and dragons here. There are musical instruments and details of armor, Jewish hats, and other costumes familiar from the period. Clothes are usually elaborate and multicolored. Regal garments are often lined with ermine. King Solomon's scepter is surmounted by a fleur-de-lys (folio 139v). There are narrative details, rare in Bibles, where pictures tend to be static. Some iconography is unusual, such as burnt offerings for Deuteronomy (folio 54v) or Queen Vashti for Esther (folio 173r). There is at least one instance of the designer's sketch for a subject drawn in plummet in the margin and never erased (Daniel in the lions' den, folio 298r).

Stained glass, Sainte-Chapelle, Paris, 13th century

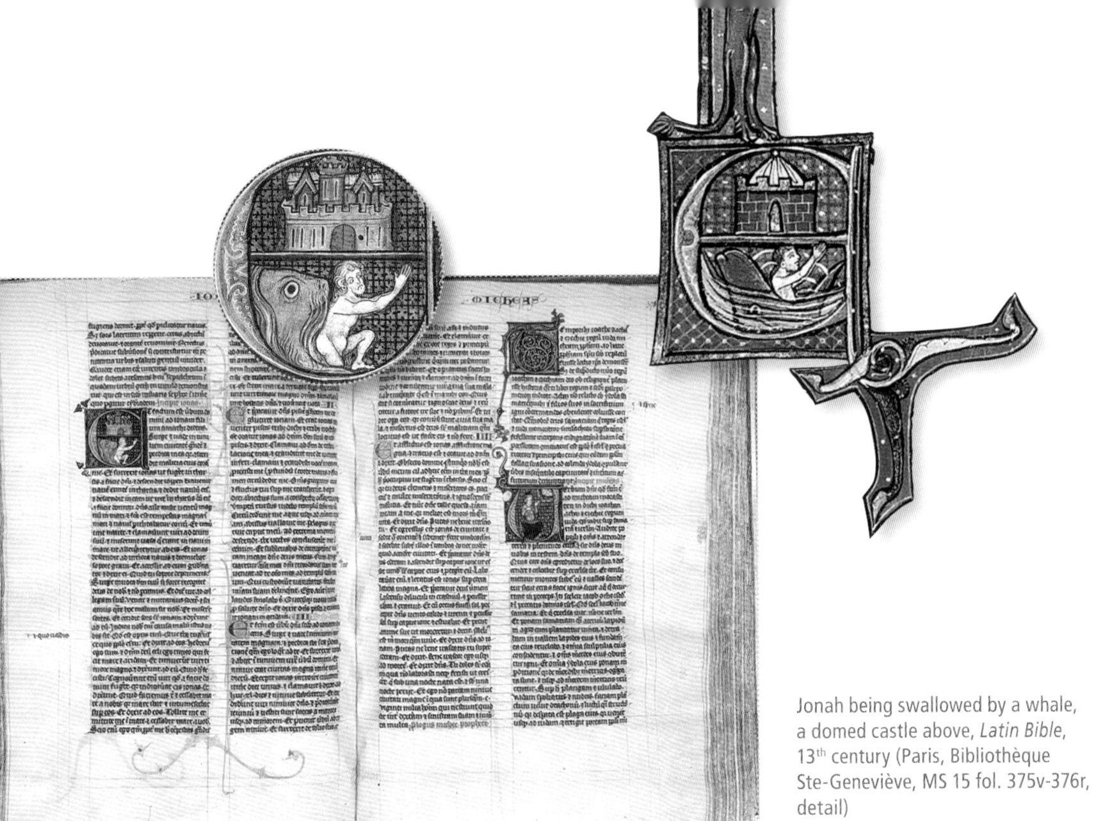

Jonah being swallowed by a whale, a domed castle above, *Latin Bible*, 13th century (Paris, Bibliothèque Ste-Geneviève, MS 15 fol. 375v-376r, detail)

Above all, the subjects for the epistles of Saint Paul are unusual and offer interpretational images selected from the text rather than the more standard author portraits of most Bibles. This complicated and interesting iconography was studied in detail by Luba Eleen (1982, pp. 118-149), who dubbed it "The Prologue Cycle," and who identified it in twelve Bibles that include the complete cycle, and an additional seven Bibles with partial cycles. Robert Branner identified an additional three (Branner 1982, pp. 194-195). Most, although not all, of these Bibles were written and illuminated in Paris, including BnF MS lat. 14397, a Bible given to the abbey of St.-Victor by Blanche of Castile (d. 1252), mother of Saint Louis. Our Bible is a significant new addition to this group.

Blanche of Castile and Louis VIII, king of France, at the bottom clerks, *Moralized Bible*, c. 1227-1234 (New York, Morgan Library & Museum, MS M.240, fol. 8r)

As recorded by Branner (pp. 238-239), some eight manuscripts can be ascribed to the workshop or circle of the Psalter of Saint Louis. They include three other exceptionally large Bibles. These are:

1. Paris, Bibliothèque Ste-Geneviève, MS 15, 346 x 240 mm. (all images digitized on the Initiale website of the IRHT).

2. Paris, Bibliothèque nationale de France, MS lat. 15185, 400 x 285 mm. (ascribed by Stones, I, i, p. 57, to a follower of the *Vie de St-Denis* Master).

3. Antwerp, Museum Plantin-Moretus, M 16.7, 310 x 220 mm. (L. Watteeuw and C. Reynolds, *Catalogue of Illuminated Manuscripts*, 2013, pp. 94-99, no. 25).

PHYSICAL DESCRIPTION

Thick modern parchment flyleaf + medieval parchment flyleaf + 457 folios on parchment (last blank) + medieval parchment flyleaf + thick modern parchment flyleaf, lacking 3 leaves, modern pencil foliation (followed here) repeats '8' and takes into account two of the three missing leaves, collation: i11 [of 12, lacking iii, a leaf after folio 2], ii16, iii-vi12, vii11 [of 12, lacking i = '75'], viii-xxv12, xxvi12 [but misbound, correct order of the leaves should be 303-5, 307-8, 306, 311, 309-10, 312-14], xxvii-xxxii12, xxxiii11 [of 12, lacking xii = '398'], xxxiv-xxxviii12, with medieval alphabetical quire signatures on last leaves 'a'-'s' (quires i-xix) beginning again 'a'-'t' (quires xx-xxxviii), mostly with medieval leaf signatures in different forms (some alphabetical and some ad hoc e.g., quire xiv), one catchword (folio 278v, end of quire xxiii); ruled in pale plummet, justification 225 x 160 mm. with slight variation, two columns of 49 lines (the Interpretations in three columns), written in dark brown ink in a fine early gothic bookhand (*textualis*), corrections to the text generally ringed in red, headings in text in red (some left blank), capitals touched in red, versal initials in Psalms and the Interpretation alternating red and blue, chapter numbers and running-titles similarly in alternating red and blue initials, 2-line chapter initials throughout in alternating red and blue with extensive penwork in the contrasting color (and spots of the first color too) usually the full height of the text block; seventy-nine large decorated initials (see below) in elaborate designs of intertwined plant stems often with lions or

dragons or grotesques and usually with long marginal extensions scrolling up and down the margins, all in full colors with delicate white tracery; seventy-seven large historiated initials (see below) in similar colors and extreme delicacy, with long marginal extensions often formed of or including dragons, usually at least the height of the text block; first page with fifteenth-century illuminated border with broad baguette and panels of colored flowers and acanthus leaves with sprays of burnished gold ivy leaves on black hairline stems, a coat-of-arms added at the foot; some medieval marginal notes and pointing hands, first page a bit battered, slight worming at extreme ends, occasional thumbing and creasing and some minor rubbing, initial on folio 32 cut out with loss of text replaced with a patch from a very similar Bible with Leviticus 20:19-25 on verso, ragged edges on extreme lower outer margins of folios 306-311, a damp stain on part of folio 378 with traces on the following pages, overall in fine state, with wide clean margins, all miniatures marked with parchment indexing tabs projecting from the outer edges of the pages; bound in nineteenth-century blind-stamped dark red-brown grained morocco over beveled wooden boards, lacking clasps but preserving a pair of metal trefoil catches on each cover (quite possibly late medieval, probably transferred from an earlier binding), parchment pastedowns, spine title gilt, corners knocked, upper joint broken. Dimensions 343 x 245 mm.

reduced

The Royal Psalter Group Bible, binding

mirabiliter transiret. Illi autem novam mor
tem invenirent. Omnis enim creatura ad suum
genus ab initio refigurabatur deserviens
tuis preceptis ut pueri tui custodirentur. Ille
sic nam nubes illorum castra obumbrabat. et ex
aqua que ante erat terra apparuit arida. et ex
mari rubro via sine impedimento. et campus
germinans de profundo nimio per quem omnis natio
transiit que tegebatur tua manu. Videntes
tua mirabilia. et monstra. Tamquam enim equi de
paverunt escam. et tamquam agni exultaverunt
magnificantes te domine qui liberasti eos. Memo
res enim adhuc erant illorum que facta fuerant quemad
(in colatu)
modum pro natione animalium produxit terra muscas
et pro piscibus eructavit fluvius multitudi
nem ranarum. Novissime autem viderunt novam
creaturam avium. cum adducti concupiscentia
postulaverunt escas epulationis. In allocu
tione enim desideriorum ascendit illis de mari ortig
gometra. et vexationes peccatoribus supervenerunt. non
sine illis que ante facta erant argumentis per vim flu
minum. Iuste enim patiebantur secundum suas nequi
tias. etenim detestabiliorem hospitalitatem
instituerunt. Alii quidem ignotos non recipie
bant advenas. alii autem bonos hospites in servi
tutem redigebant. et non solum hoc sed et alius quidem
erat respectus illorum quoniam inviti recipiebant
extraneos. Qui autem cum letitia receperunt hos qui
eisdem usi erant iustitiis. sevissimis afflixe
runt doloribus. Percussi sunt autem cecitate. sicut illi in foribus
iusti cum subitaneis operti essent tenebris unus
quisque transitum ostii sui querebat. In se enim elementa con
vertuntur sicut in organo qualitatis sonus immutatur. et
omnia suum sonum custodiunt. Unde estimari ex ipso
certo visu potest. Agrestia enim in aquatica convertebantur
tur. et quecumque erant natantia in terram transiebant.
Ignis in aqua valebat supra suam virtutem. et aqua extin
guentis nature obliviscebatur. Flamme e contrari
o corruptibilium animalium non vexaverunt carnes co
ambulantium. nec dissolvebant illam que facile dis
solvebatur sicut glacies bonam escam. In omnibus enim
magnificasti populum tuum domine et honorasti et non de
spexisti in omni tempore et in omni loco assistens eis. *In*
[M]ultorum *cipit prologus in librum ecclesiastici*
nobis et magnorum per legem et pro
phetas aliisque qui secuti sunt
illos sapientia demonstrata est.
in quibus oportet laudare israel
doctrine et sapientie causa. quia non solum
ipsos loquentes necesse est esse peritos. sed et extraneos
posse et dicentes et conscribentes doctissimos fi
eri. Avus meus ihesus postquam se amplius dedit
ad diligentiam lectionis legis et prophetarum et alio
rum librorum qui a nobis a parentibus nostris tradi
ti sunt. voluit et ipse scribere aliquid horum que
ad doctrinam et sapientiam pertinent. ut desideran
tes discere et illorum periti facti magis magisque atten
dant animo. et confirmentur ad legitimam vitam.
Hortor itaque venire vos cum benivolentia et
et attentiori studio lectionem facere. et veniam
habere in illis quibus videmur sequentes ymaginem
sapientie deficere in verborum compositione. Nam de
ficiunt verba hebraica quando fuerint translata
ad aliam linguam. Non autem solum hec. sed et ipsa
lex et prophete. ceteraque librorum non parvam habent dif
ferentiam quando inter se dicuntur. Nam in octa
vo et xxx. anno temporibus ptholomei eurgetis regis
postquam perveni in egyptum. et cum multum temporis
ibi fecissem moram. ibi inveni libros relic
tos non parvae neque contemptibilis doctrine.
Itaque bonum et necessarium putavi et aliquam ad
dere diligentiam et laborem interpretandi istum
librum. et multa vigilia attuli doctrinam in spa
tio temporis ad illa que ad finem ducunt librum
istum dare. et illis qui volunt animum intendere
et discere quemadmodum oporteat instituere mores qui
secundum legem domini proposuerint vitam agere.
Incipit liber ecclesiasticus
[O]mnis sapientia a domino deo
est. et cum illo fuit semper
et est ante evum. Harenam
maris et pluvie guttas.
et dies seculi quis dinume
ravit. Altitudinem celi et lati
tudinem terre et profundum abys
si quis dimensus est. Sapientiam dei precedentem omni
a quis investigavit. Prior omnium creata est sa
pientia. et intellectus prudentie ab evo. Fons
sapientie verbum dei in excelsis. et ingressus illius
mandata eterna. Radix sapientie cui revelata est.
et astutias illius quis agnovit. Discipli
na sapientie cui revelata est et manifestata. et mul
tiplicationem ingressus illius quis intelle
xit. Unus est altissimus creator omnium omnipotens et rex
potens et metuendus nimis sedens super thro
num illius et dominans deus. Ipse creavit illam
in spiritu sancto. et vidit et dinumeravit et mensus est. et ef
fudit illam super omnia opera sua. et super omnem car

reduced

TEXT

The manuscript opens "*Incipit epistola sancti ieronimi presbiteri ad paulinum de omnibus divine hystorie libris*, Frater ambrosius...." It comprises the conventional Paris Bible in what Neil Ker called "the usual order" for the thirteenth century (*Medieval Manuscripts in British Libraries*, 1969, p. 96), with the prologues numbered by Stegmüller as follows: General prologue no. 284 (folio 1r); prologue and opening of Genesis lacking; Joshua no. 311 (folio 66v); I Kings no. 323 (folio 85r); I Chronicles no. 328 (folio 129v); II Chronicles no. 327 (folio 139r); I Ezra no. 330 (folio 151v); Tobit no. 332 (folio 165r); Judith no. 335 (folio 168v); Esther no. 341 (folio 173r); Job nos. 344 and 357 (folio 177v); Proverbs no. 457 (folio 208r); Ecclesiastes no. 462 (folio 215r); Wisdom no. 468 (folio 219r); Isaiah no. 482 (folio 239r); Jeremiah no. 487 (folio 256r); Baruch no. 491 (folio 277v); Ezekiel no. 492 (folio 280r); Daniel no. 494 (folio 297v); Minor Prophets no. 500 (folio 303r); Hosea no. 507 (folio 303r); Joel nos. 511 and 510 (folio 308v); Amos nos. 515, 512 and 513 (folios 306v and 311r, the gathering is disordered); Obadiah no. 519 and variant prologue "Esau filius ysaac ..." (folio 310r); Jonah nos. 524 and 521 (folio 310v); Micah no. 526 (folio 312v); Nahum no. 528 (folio 313r); Habakkuk nos. 531 and 530 (folios 314v and 315r); Zephaniah no. 534 (folio 316r); Haggai no. 538 (folio 317r); Zechariah no. 539 (folio 317v); Malachi no. 543 (folio 320v); I Maccabees nos. 547, 553 and 551 (folios 321v and 322r); Matthew nos. 590 and 589 (folios 339v and 340r); Mark no. 607 (folio 350v); Luke no. 620 (folio 357v); John no. 624 (folio 369r); Romans no. 677 and variant prologue (actually a capitula list) "Paulus servus ihesu fidem Romanorum..." (folio 377v); I Corinthians no. 685 (folio 382r); II Corinthians no. 699 (folio 386v); Galatians no. 707 (folio 389v); Ephesians no. 715 (folio 390v); Philippians no. 728 (folio 392r); Colossians no. 736 (folio 393r); I Thessalonians no. 747 (folio 394r); II Thessalonians no. 752 (folio 395r); I Timothy no. 765 (folio 395v); II Timothy no. 772 (folio 396v); Titus no. 780 (folio 398v); prologue and openings of Philemon and Hebrews lacking; Acts no. 640 (folio 401v); Canonical or Catholic Epistles no. 809 (folio 413r); and Apocalypse or Revelation no. 839 (folio 418v). These are followed by the Interpretations of Hebrew Names in the standard version beginning "Aaz apprehendens...," all ending on folio 457v, "eorum, Expliciunt interpretationes hebraiorum nominum".

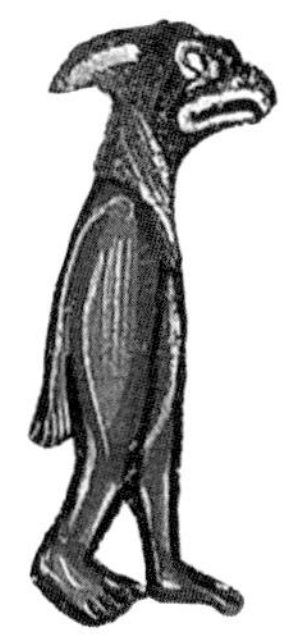

Folio 224v, Ecclesia, a queen standing in a gothic church holding a cross with banner and a gold chalice, Ecclesiasticus

ILLUMINATION

The historiated initials here are:

1. Saint Jerome writing, seated at a desk in a gothic enclosure, 7 lines, 33 x 35 mm., with full-length descender terminating in a biting dragon, folio 1r, general prologue.

2. Moses receiving the Law from God, Moses horned, God passing a gold tablet from the sky, 5 lines, 23 x 28 mm., with extension to 180 mm. high, folio 18v, Exodus.

3. The Lord speaking to Moses, 7 lines, 30 x 37 mm., with extension to 115 mm. high, folio 41v, Numbers.

4. Moses advising the Israelites on the procedure for burnt offerings, 7 lines, 31 x 32 mm., with extension to 250 mm. high, folio 54v, Deuteronomy.

5. The Lord speaking to Joshua, 7 lines, 33 x 34 mm., with extension to 240 mm. high including two grotesques with human heads, folio 66v, Joshua.

6. Elimelech and his wife Naomi travelling to the country of Moab with bags of possessions over their shoulders, 24 lines (an initial 'I'), 112 x 13 mm., with extension to 246 mm. high, folio 83v, Ruth.

7. The beheading of Ophni and Phineas at the battle of Aphek, 7 lines, 30 x 31 mm., with extension to 256 mm. high, folio 85v, I Kings (I Samuel).

8. King David ordering the beheading of the Amalekite, 8 lines, 37 x 33 mm., with extension to 255 mm. high, folio 97v, II Kings (II Samuel).

9. Abishag being brought to David as he lies in bed in old age, 7 lines, 31 x 37 mm., with extension to 206 mm. high, folio 107v, III Kings (I Kings).

10. King Ahaziah falling from a tower of his palace in Samaria, 5 lines (at foot of page, extending into lower margin), 30 x 33 mm., with extension to 268 mm. high, folio 119r, IV Kings (II Kings).

11. The descendants of Adam, several wearing tall Jewish hats, 7 lines, 33 x 35 mm., with extension to 243 mm. high, folio 130r, I Chronicles.

12. King Solomon enthroned, with sword and scepter, 7 lines, 33 x 34 mm., with extension to 208 mm. high, folio 139v, II Chronicles.

13. The Lord holding a book and Cyrus the king of Persia ordering the building of the Temple, set in a gothic building, 35 lines (a tall letter 'I'), 157 x 14 mm., with extension to 260 mm. high, folio 152r, I Ezra.

14. Nehemiah bringing wine to King Artaxerxes, 4 lines (at foot of page, extending into lower margin), 27 x 31 mm., with extension to 148 mm. high, folio 155r, Nehemiah.

15. Josias keeping the Passover in the temple in Jerusalem, 8 lines, 35 x 35 mm., with extension to 210 mm. high, folio 160r, II Ezra (I Esdras).

16. Tobit in bed being blinded by the droppings of swallows, 7 lines, 30 x 35 mm., with extension to 155 mm. high including a hooded grotesque, folio 165r, Tobit.

Folio 256r, the stoning of Jeremiah, Jeremiah

tionem ⁊ uirtutem simul consumentur. dicit
dñs. Ego aũt opa eoꝝ ⁊ cogitatões eoꝝ uenio ut co
gregem cũ omĩbꝫ gentibꝫ ⁊ linguis ⁊ uenient
⁊ uidebunt glãm meam. ⁊ ponã in eis signũ.
⁊ mittam ex eis qui saluati fuint ad gentes ĩ
mare. in affricam ⁊ ludiam tenentes sagittã ĩ
ytaliam ⁊ greciam ad insulas longe ad eos q̃
nõ audierunt de me ⁊ nõ uiderunt glãm me
am. ⁊ anũtiabunt glãm meã gentibꝫ ⁊ addu
cent omnes gentes frẽs urõs de cunctis gentibꝫ
donũ dño in equis ⁊ q̃drigis ⁊ ĩ lecticis ⁊ ĩ mu
lis ⁊ in carrucis ad montem scm̃ meũ ierlm̃
dicit dñs. Quomõ si inferant filii isrł munus
ĩ uase mundo in domũ dñi. Et assumam ex
eis in sacdotes ⁊ leuitas dicit dñs. Quĩa sicut
celi noui ⁊ t̃ra noua q̃ ego facio stare corã me
dicit dñs. sic stabit semẽ urm̃ ⁊ nomẽ urm̃. Et
erit mensis ex mẽse. ⁊ sabbm̃ ex sabbo. ueniet
omĩs caro ut adoret coram facie mea dicit do
minus. Et egredientur ⁊ uidebunt cadauera
uiroꝝ qui p̃uaricati sũt in me. Vermis eoꝝ nõ
morietur ⁊ ignis eoꝝ nõ extinguetur ⁊ erunt
usq; ad sacietatem uisionis omĩ carni. Incipit
prologus ieremie prophete

Ieremias ꝓpha
cui hic ꝓlogus scribitur sermone qui
dem apud hebreos ysaie ⁊ osee ⁊ quibusdam
aliis ꝓphis uidetur ẽe rusticior. sed sen
sibꝫ par ẽ quippe qui eodẽ spũ ꝓphauit.
porro simplicitas eloquii de loco ei ĩ quo
natus ẽ accidit. Fuit enĩ anathotites q̃
ẽ usq; hodie uiculus tribꝫ ab ierosolimis
distãs milibꝫ. sacdos ⁊ ĩ matris utõ scĩfi
catus. Virginitate sua euangelicũ uirũ
xpi ẽẽ dedicans. Hic uaticinari exorsus
ẽ puer ⁊ captiuitatẽ urbis ac iudee nõ so
lum spũ s; ⁊ oclis carnis intuitus ẽ. quõ
x tribꝫ isrł assyrii ĩ medos transtulerũt.
ignotas t̃ras eoꝝ colonie gentiũ possidebãt.
Vnde in iuda tm̃ ⁊ beniamin ꝓphauit
⁊ ciuitatis sue ruinas q̃druplici plan
xit alphabeto qđ nos mensure metri u̾si
bꝫq; reddidimus. p̃terea ordinẽ uisionũ
qui apud grecos ⁊ latinos oĩno ꝯfusus ẽ
ad pristinam fidem correximus. Libꝝ
aũt baruch notarii eius qui apud hebre
os nec legitur nec hẽtur p̃termisimus
ꝓ his omĩbꝫ maledicta ab emulis p̃sto
lantes quibꝫ me necẽe ẽ p singula o
puscla r̃ndẽ. ⁊ hoc facio q̃ uos cogi

ex sacdotibꝫ

tis o paula ⁊ eustochium. certum ad compẽ
dium mali rectius fuerat modum furori
eoꝝ silentio meo ponẽ q̃m cotidie noui ali
quid scriptitãte ĩ insaniam inuidoꝝ ꝓuocare.

Incipit ieremias propheta

Verba ieremie filii helchie
de sacdotibꝫ qui fuerunt
in anathot. in t̃ra benia
min. quod factũ ẽ u̾bum
dñi ad eum in diebꝫ iosie
filii amon regis iuda in
t̃cio decimo anno regni
eius. Et factũ ẽ in diebꝫ io
achim regis iuda filii iosie usq; ad consũma
tionẽ undecimi anni sedechie filii iosie regis
iuda usq; ad transmigratiõem ierlm̃ ĩ mense
q̃nto. Et factũ est u̾bum dñi ad me dicens. Pri
usq̃m te formarem in utõ noui te. ⁊ antequã
exires de uulua. sc̃ificaui te. ⁊ ꝓpham ĩ genti
bꝫ dedi te. Et dixi. a. a. a. dñe dš. Ecce nescio loqui
q̃ puer ego sum. Et dixit dñs ad me. Noli dic̃
q̃ puer sum. q̃m ad omĩa q̃ mittam te ibis. ⁊
uniũsa q̃cumq; mandauo tibi loq̃ris. Ne ti
meas a facie eoꝝ. q̃ ego sum tecum. ut eruã
te dicit dñs. ⁊ misit dñs manũ suã ⁊ tetigit
os meũ. Et dixit dñs ad me. Ecce dedi u̾ba mea
in ore tuo. ecce constitui te hodie sup̃ gentes ⁊ sup̃
regna. ut euellas. ⁊ destruas. ⁊ disꝑdas ⁊ dissipes
⁊ edifices ⁊ plantes. Et factũ ẽ u̾bum dñi ad me
dicens. Quid tu uides ieremia. ⁊ dixi. Virgã
uigilantem ego uideo. Et dixit dñs ad me. Bene
uidisti. q̃ q̃ uigilabo ego sup̃ u̾bo meo ut faciã
illud. Et factũ ẽ u̾bum dñi scđo ad me dicens. Quid
tu uides ieremia. ⁊ dixi. Ollam succensam ego
uideo ⁊ faciem eius a facie aquilonis. Et dixit
dñs ad me. Ab aquilone pandetur omne malũ
sup̃ omĩs habitatores t̃re. q̃ ecce ego conuocabo
omĩs cognationes regnoꝝ aquilonis ait dñs.
Et uenient ⁊ ponent unusquisq; soliũ suũ in
introitu portarũ ierlm̃. ⁊ sup̃ omĩs muros eius ĩ
circuitu ⁊ sup̃ uniũsas urbes iuda ⁊ loquar iudi
cia mea cum eis sup̃ omĩ malicia eoꝝ qui dereli
querunt me ⁊ libauerunt diis alienis ⁊ adora
uerunt opus manuũ suaꝝ. Tu ergo accinge
lumbos tuos. ⁊ surge ⁊ loquere ad eos omĩa
q̃ ego p̃cipio tibi. Ne formides a facie eoꝝ. nec
enĩ timere te faciam uultus eoꝝ. Ego quip
pe dedi te hodie in ciuitatem munitam ⁊ ĩ
columpnã ferream ⁊ ĩ murũ eneũ sup̃ omnẽ

reduced

17. Judith, attended by her maid, cutting off the head of King Holofernes as he lies in bed in his tent, 8 lines, 36 x 38 mm., with extension to 130 mm. high, folio 168v, Judith.

18. Queen Vashti standing looking up at King Ahasuerus in the citadel of Susa, 25 lines (a tall letter 'I'), 124 x 14 mm., with extension to 240 mm. high, folio 173r, Esther.

19. Job on the dung heap in conversation with his wife dressed as a queen and with her attendants, 8 lines, 35 x 40 mm., with extension to 218 mm. high, folio 178r, Job.

20. King David playing the harp in his palace, 9 lines, 42 x 37 mm., with extension to 235 mm. high, folio 186v, Psalm 1.

21. Samuel anointing King David, 7 lines, 31 x 37 mm., with extension to 226 mm. high, folio 190r, Psalm 26 (27).

22. David in his palace looking up at God and pointing to his own mouth, 7 lines, 31 x 39 mm., with extension to 137 mm. high, folio 192r, Psalm 38 (39).

23. A soldier in armor, presumably Goliath, 7 lines, 31 x 35 mm., with dragon extension to 93 mm. high, folio 194r, Psalm 51 (52).

24. A fool, with stick and ball, 8 lines, 38 x 40 mm., with dragon extension to 148 mm., also folio 194r, Psalm 52 (53).

25. David standing half-length in green sea, calling to God appearing above, 9 lines, 40 x 40 mm., with extension to 254 mm. high, folio 196r, Psalm 68 (69).

26. David seated in a great chair reaching up to play bells above his head, 9 lines, 40 x 41 mm., with extension to 224 mm. high, folio 198v, Psalm 80 (81).

27. Three priests singing from a manuscript on a lectern in a gothic church, 8 lines, 36 x 38 mm., with extension to 243 mm. high, folio 200v, Psalm 96 (97).

28. The Trinity, the Father and Son seated side by side with the Holy Dove above them, 8 lines, 37 x 37 mm., with extension to 240 mm. high, folio 203r, Psalm 109 (110).

29. King Solomon seated with a birch rod looking down at a diminutive child with a book, doubtless his son Rehoboam, 8 lines, 38 x 34 mm., with extension to 240 mm. high, folio 208r, Proverbs.

30. King Solomon again seated with a birch rod looking down at a child with a book, 8 lines, 36 x 40 mm., with extension to 233 mm. high, folio 215v, Ecclesiastes.

31. The Virgin and Child, Mary crowned, seated on a throne, 7 lines, 32 x 39 mm., with extension to 240 mm. high, folio 218r, Song of Songs.

32. King Solomon giving the sword of justice to a young man, 8 lines, 36 x 37 mm., with extension to 238 mm. high, folio 219v, Wisdom.

33. Ecclesia, a queen standing in a gothic church holding a cross with banner and a gold chalice, 8 lines, 37 x 37 mm., with extension to 229 mm. high, folio 224v, Ecclesiasticus.

34. Isaiah tied to a post with his head being sawn by two men, 9 lines, 40 x 40 mm., with extension to 230 mm. high, folio 239r, Isaiah.

Folio 280r, the vision of Ezekiel, who lies in bed as haloed heads appear above him with the man, lion, ox and eagle, Ezekiel

sunt a deo perambulare universum orbem praeceptum quod imperatum est eis. Ignis etiam missus desuper ut consumat montes et silvas facit quod praeceptum est ei. Haec autem neque speciebus neque virtutibus uni eorum similia sunt. Unde neque estimandum est neque dicendum illos esse deos quando non possunt neque iudicium iudicare neque facere hominibus. Scientes itaque quod non sunt dii ne ergo timueritis eos. Neque enim regibus maledicent neque benedicent. Signa etiam in caelo gentibus non ostendunt neque ut sol lucebunt neque illuminabunt ut luna. Bestiae meliores sunt illis quae possunt sub tectum fugere ac prodesse sibi. Nullo itaque modo nobis est manifestum quia sunt dii propter quod non timeatis eos. Nam sicut in cucumerario formido nihil custodit ita sunt dii eorum lignei et argentei et inaurati. Eodem modo et in orto spina alba supra quam omnis avis sedet. Similiter et mortuo proiecto in tenebris similes sunt dii illorum lignei et inaurati et argentati. A purpura quoque et marmore quae super illos teneant scietis itaque quia non sunt dii. Ipsi etiam postremo comeduntur et erit in opprobrium in regione. Melior est homo iustus qui non habet simulachra nam erit longe ab opprobriis.

Incipit prologus sancti Ieronimi in Ezechiel prophetam

Ezechiel propheta cum Ioachim rege Iuda captivus ductus est in Babilonem. Ibique his qui cum eo captivi fuerant prophetavit paenitentibus quod ad Ieremiae vaticinium se ultro adversariis tradidissent et viderent adhuc urbem Ierosolimam stare quam ille casuram esse predixerat. Tricesimo autem etatis sue anno et captivitatis quinto exorsus est ad captivos loqui et eodem tempore licet posterior hic in Chaldea Ieremias in Iudea prophetavit. Sermo eius nec satis disertus nec admodum rusticus est sed ex utroque medie temperatus. Sacerdos et ipse sicut et Ieremias principia voluminis et finem magnis habens obscuritatibus involuta. Sed et vulgata eius editio non multum distat ab hebraico. Unde satis miror quid causae extiterit ut si eosdem in ceteris libris habemus interpretes in aliis eadem in aliis diversa transtulerint. Legite ergo et hunc iuxta translationem nostram quia per cola scriptus et commata manifestiorem sensum legentibus tribuit. Si autem amici mei exhinc subsannaverint dicite eis quod nemo eos compellat ut scribant. Sed vereor ne illis eveniat quod graece significantius dicitur ut vocentur fagoloidori hoc est apud nos manducantes senectutem.

Incipit Ezechiel propheta.

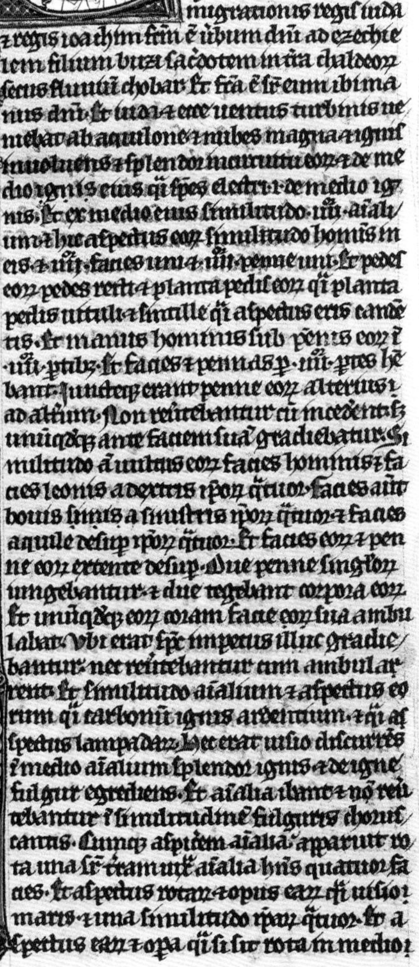

Et factum est in tricesimo anno in quarto mense quinta die mensis cum essem in medio captivorum iuxta fluvium Chobar aperti sunt caeli et vidi visiones Dei. In quinta mensis ipse est annus quintus transmigrationis regis Ioachim factum est verbum Domini ad Ezechielem filium Buzi sacerdotem in terra Chaldeorum secus flumen Chobar et facta est super eum ibi manus Domini. Et vidi et ecce ventus turbinis veniebat ab aquilone et nubes magna et ignis involvens et splendor in circuitu eius et de medio eius quasi species electri id est de medio ignis. Et in medio eius similitudo quattuor animalium et hic aspectus eorum similitudo hominis in eis. Et quattuor facies uni et quattuor pennae uni. Et pedes eorum pedes recti et planta pedis eorum quasi planta pedis vituli et scintillae quasi aspectus aeris candentis. Et manus hominis sub pennis eorum in quattuor partibus et facies et pennas per quattuor partes habebant. Iunctaeque erant pennae eorum alterius ad alterum. Non revertebantur cum incederent sed unumquodque ante faciem suam gradiebatur. Similitudo autem vultus eorum facies hominis et facies leonis a dextris ipsorum quattuor facies autem bovis a sinistris ipsorum quattuor et facies aquilae desuper ipsorum quattuor. Et facies eorum et pennae eorum extentae desuper. Duae pennae singulorum iungebantur et duae tegebant corpora eorum. Et unumquodque eorum coram facie sua ambulabat. Ubi erat impetus spiritus illuc gradiebantur nec revertebantur cum ambularent. Et similitudo animalium et aspectus eorum quasi carbonum ignis ardentium et quasi aspectus lampadarum. Haec erat visio discurrens in medio animalium splendor ignis et de igne fulgur egrediens. Et animalia ibant et non revertebantur in similitudinem fulguris choruscantis. Cumque aspicerem animalia apparuit rota una super terram iuxta animalia habens quattuor facies. Et aspectus rotarum et opus earum quasi visio maris et una similitudo ipsarum quattuor. Et aspectus earum et opera quasi sit rota in medio

reduced

tuũ inde detraham te dicit dñs. Si fures introis-
issent ad te si latrones p noctem quomõ contic-
uisses. Nonne furati essent sufficientia sibi. Si uin-
demiatores introissent ad te. Numquid saltē
reliquissent tibi racemos. Quõ scrutati sunt
esau inuestigauerunt abscondita eius. Usque ad
terminũ emiserunt te. Omnes uiri federis tui
illuserunt tibi. Inualuerunt aduersum te uiri
pacis tue. Qui comederunt tecum ponent in-
sidias subter te. Non ē prudentia ī eo. Numquid
te nõ in die illa dicit dñs pdam sapientes ydu-
mea. et prudentiam de monte esau. Et time-
bunt fortes tui meridie. ut intereat uir de monte esau. ppt interfectionem. et ppt iniquitatē fratrem tuum iacob operiet te confusio et peribis ineternũ. In
die qua stabas aduersus eum quando capiebant alie-
ni exercitum eius et extranei egrediebantur
portas eius et sup ierslm mittebant sortē. tu quoque e-
fris tui ras quasi unus ex eis. Et nõ despicies ī die peregri-
nationis eius. et nõ letaberis sup filios iude ī die
pditionis eorum et nõ magnificabis os tuũ ī die
illa angustie. neque egredieris portam ppli mei
in die ruine eorum. Neque despicies et tu ī malis eius
ī die uastitatis illius et nõ emitteris aduersus
exercitum eius in die uastitatis illius. Neque sta-
bis in exitibus ut interficias eos qui fugerint
et nõ concludes reliquos eius in die tribulati-
onis. Quoniam iuxta ē dies dñi sup omnes gentes. Sicut fe-
cisti fiat tibi. retributionem tuam conuertet ī caput tuũ. Quomodo enim bibisti sup montē scm meũ. bibēt
omnes gentes iugiter et bibent et absorbebunt. et
erunt quasi nõ sint. Et ī monte syon erit salua-
tio et erit scs. Et possidebit domus iacob eos qui
possederant se. Et erit domus iacob ignis et
domus ioseph flamma et domus esau stipula.
Et succendentur ī eis et deuorabunt eos et non
erunt reliquie domus esau. quia dñs locutus ē. Et here-
ditabunt hii qui ad austrum sunt montem
esau et qui ī campestribus philistiim et possidebunt regionē effraym et regionē samarie et beniamin
possidebit galaad. transmigratio exercitus hui-
filiorum isrl. Omnia loca chananeorum usque ad sarep-
ta sydoniorum et transmigratio ierlm que ī bospho-
ro ē possidebit ciuitates austri. Et ascendent
saluatores ī montē syon iudicare montē esa-
u et erit dño regnũ. amen. Plogus sup ionam

Sanctum ionam hebrei affirmant
filiũ fuisse mulieris uidue sarep-
tane quem helyas ppha mortuũ suscita-
uit matre postea dicente ad eũ. Nunc cogno-
ui quia uir dei es tu et uerbum dei ī ore tuo ē ueri-
tas. Ob hanc causam et ipsum puerum sic uocatum
amathi. Amathi enim in nostra lingua ueritatem sonat. et ex eo quod uerum helyas locutus
ē ille qui suscitatus ē filius esse dicitur ueritatis.
Ideo de ueritate columba nascitur. quia iona
columbam sonat. In condempnatione autem
isrl ionas ad gentes mittitur. quia niniuea
gente penitentiam illi ī malicia pseuerant. Temporibus quippe ieroboe regis isrl. qui deo de-
relicto ē suo ppło ī samaria ydolis sacrificab-
at ionam pphetam fuisse. uti liber regum
indicat. testatur. Is cum ppha illuminatur
pectores ciuitatis niniue misam dei consecutu-
ros uideret. ne falsa uidetur predicare ad denun-
ciandum interitum eiusdem ciuitatis ire nolebat.
Nam sicut deus ad abraham de impietate sodom-
orum et gomorreorum locutus ē clamor sodomo-
rum et gomorreorum puenit ad me. ita et de
niniue dicit. eo quod ascenderit clamor malici-
e eius ad deum. et quia sententia dei de sodomis fratrem mi-
nime reuocata ē. ita et ionas aduersum nini-
uen placatam sententiam reuocari nolebat diui-
ne dispensationis ignarus. qui salutem
hominum ad se conuertentium magis uult quam interitum. Hoc illi accidit quod et scõ helyseo qui filium sunamitis mulieris mortuũ ignorau-
it. Ideo a conspectu dei ionas fugere se puta-
bat humanũ aliquid passus dicente dauid
Quo ibo a spiritu tuo. et quo a facie tua fugiã.
Ionas columba. Incipit alius plogus
et dolens filius amathi qui fuit de geth
que ē in ophir ad gentium preconium mittitur.
missus contempnit. contempnens fugit.
fugiens dormit. ppt quem periclitatur na-
uis. Sed sors latentem reperit. cetus abiec-
tum deuorauit. ppt quem et orantem reuomu-
it. Reiectus predicauit subuersionem. Sed con-
tristatur in penitentia urbis. et salutem gentium ī-
uidet. Gaudet ī edere uirentis umbracu-
lo et dolet subito arescentis cuius sepulchrũ
ī quadam urbicula geth ī uiculo demonstratur.
que est in secundo miliario sephorim itinere quo p-
gitur tyberiadem. Incipit ionas ppha.

Et factum ē uerbum dñi ad ionam filium amathi dicens. Surge et ua-
de in niniuen ciuitatem grandem.
et predica in ea. Quia ascendit ma-

reduced

Folios 310v-311r, Jonah being swallowed by a whale, a domed castle above, doubtless Nineveh, Jonah; a prophet with a scroll and God above, Amos

35. The stoning of Jeremiah, 9 lines, 41 x 38 mm., with extension to 242 mm. high, folio 256r, Jeremiah.

36. Jeremiah seated with his head in his hands beside the ruins of Jerusalem, 4 lines, 20 x 23 mm., with extension to 205 mm. high, folio 275v, Lamentations.

37. A prophet seated in thought at a scribe's desk built of brick, 6 lines, 30 x 38 mm., extended below by a hooded grotesque with hooves to 62 mm. high, folio 277v, Baruch.

38. Baruch again seated at his brickwork desk, 6 lines with indented descender bringing the height to 20 lines, 28 x 28 mm., with extension to 247 mm. high, folio 279r, described as Baruch again with prologue but actually a continuation of the same text with the opening of Baruch 6.

39. The vision of Ezekiel, who lies in bed as haloed heads appear above him with the man, lion, ox and eagle, 8 lines, 37 x 39 mm., with extension to 240 mm. high including a grotesque donkey, folio 280r, Ezekiel.

40. Daniel in the lions' den, with two lions laying their heads on his lap, 8 lines, 37 x 43 mm., with extension to 240 mm. high, folio 298r, Daniel.

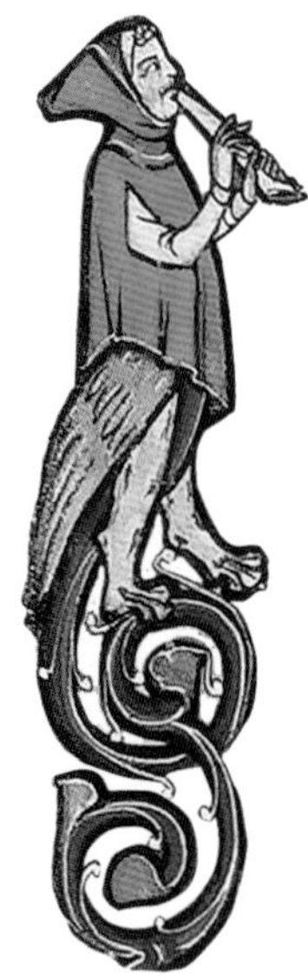

41. A prophet standing in a church holding a scroll, God above, 8 lines, 36 x 39 mm., with extension to 152 mm. high, folio 306r, Joel.

42. A prophet holding a scroll looking up to God, 8 lines, 36 x 36 mm., with extension to 87mm. high joining into that for the initial above, folio 310r, Obadiah.

43. Jonah being swallowed by a whale, a domed castle above, doubtless Nineveh, 4 line (at foot of page, extending into lower margin), 27 x 30 mm., folio 310v, Jonah.

44. A prophet with a scroll and God above, 7 lines, 32 x 34 mm., with extension to 225 mm. high, folio 311r, Amos.

45. A prophet with a book and God above, 6 lines, 28 x 37 mm., with extension to 132 mm. high, folio 312v, Micah.

46. A prophet speaking with God, 7 lines, 33 x 37 mm., with extension formed of an ostrich and a grotesque to 92 mm. high, folio 314r, Nahum.

47. A prophet with a book and God above, 7 lines, 32 x 37 mm., with extension formed of a hooded grotesque, folio 315r, Habakkuk.

48. A prophet with a scroll and God above, 7 lines, 32 x 34 mm., with extension to 230 mm. high, folio 316r, Zephaniah.

49. A prophet speaking with God, 35 lines (an initial 'I'), 157 x 12 mm., with extension to 280 mm. high, folio 317r, Haggai.

50. A prophet standing in a church, 39 lines (an initial 'I'), 180 x 18 mm., with extension to 270 mm. high, folio 318r, Zechariah.

51. A prophet with a scroll and God above, 7 lines, 30 x 33 mm., with extension including a long-necked bird (perhaps a crane) holding a pebble in its beak, folio 320v, Malachi.

Folio 317r, a prophet speaking with God, initial 'I', Haggai

Gaudebit super te in leticia, silebit in dilectione tua, ex
ultabit super te in laude. Nugas qui a lege recesserant
congregabo, quia ex te erant, ut non ultra habeas super
eis obprobrium. Ecce ego interficiam omnes qui af
flixerunt te in tempore illo, et salvabo claudican
tem, et eam que eiecta fuerat congregabo, et ponam eos
in laudem et in nomen in omni terra confusionis eorum. In
tempore illo quo adducam vos, et in tempore quo congrega
bo vos. Dabo enim vos in nomen et in laudem omnibus
populis terre, cum convertero captivitatem vestram coram ocu
lis vestris, dicit dominus. Incipit prologus Aggei prophete.

Ieremias propheta ob causam periurii Sedechie regis
ut in hystoria libri secundi Paralipomenon indicatur
qui fidem promissam Nabuchodonosor regi Chaldeorum
non servaverat, populum Israel refert cum memora
to rege Israel expugnata Ierusalem captivum in
Babilonem fuisse perductum. Sed cum populus
memoratus multis temporibus ydolis servien
do et effusione sanguinis innocentium se gra
viter inplicasset, volens quoque deus generationem u
niversam eiusdem populi ob causas memoratas
penitus deperire, lxx annorum captivitatem in
eundem populum in terra Chaldeorum statuit susti
nere, hac ratione ut completo numero annorum no
vus populus inmunis a memoratis peccatis in
ad renovationem Ierusalem perveniret. Sexa
gesimo itaque secundo anno regno Chalde
orum subverso, cum adhuc octo anni ad reg
nandum restabant, cap. viii. visio Danie
lis ostendit propter causam sacrilegii, quod in eadem
visione continetur, fuisse extinctum. Darius
qui medis imperabat ut septima visio Danie
lis ostendit memoratorum regno successit. Cuius
primo anno regni ut decima visio ostendit
Daniel supputatis annis videns appropinqua
re tempus reversionis quod per Ieremiam fuerat pro
missa, orans tam pro se quam pro populo eandem vi
sionem a deo postulabat impleri. Sicut per Gabri
elem angelum in eandem visione invenies preces eius
universa esse completa deus eduxit. Nam mori
ente supradicto rege Medorum et succedente regno eorum
Cyro rege Persarum permissione dei completa per eun
dem regem populum Israel in Ierusalem reductum hys
toria libri secundi Paralipomenon et initium Esdre confirma
vit. Cumque a populo Israel et a senioribus templum
dei edificari cepisset, mortuo Cyro rege Persarum ac
regnante Dario rege Persarum, qui memorato suc
cesserat, vicine gentes civitatis Ierusalem ut idem
Esdras refert restaurationem templi et civitatis
impedire ceperunt. Quia tunc decimus populus Israel res
taurationem supradicti templi domini necdum promissi
one inventam concessam esse credebant. Propter quod in secundo
anno regni memorati Darii regis Persarum Aggeus
propheta a deo missus ad Zorobabel qui de tribu Iuda erat qui potestatem
regni sui susceperat,
erat, et Ihesum filium Iosedech summum sacerdotem admo
net ut credant completo numero annorum tempus res
taurationis Ierusalem advenisse. Hoc addito nec in
credulitatem populi vellent mutari de quo deus dicit
per eum: Populus hic dicit: Nondum venit tempus ut e
dificetur domus dei. Omnia autem que textu huius prophetie con
tinentur reversionem populi, edificationem templi, re
novationem civitatis, observantiam sacerdotalem
et initium regnorum exterorum significant. Incipit Age
us propheta.

In anno secundo Darii
regis Persarum in mense vi in die una mensis
factum est verbum domini in manu Aggei prophete ad
Zorobabel filium Salathiel ducem Iuda
et ad Ihesum filium Iosedech sacerdotem magnum
dicens. Hec dicit dominus exercituum dicens: Populus
iste dicit: Nondum venit tempus domus
domini edificande. Et factum est verbum domini in ma
nu Aggei prophete dicens: Numquid tempus
vobis est ut habitetis in domibus laqueatis, et domus
ista deserta? Et nunc hec dicit dominus exercituum:
Ponite corda vestra super vias vestras. Semina
stis multum et intulistis parum; comedistis
et non estis saciati; bibistis et non estis inebri
ati; operuistis vos et non estis calefacti; et
qui mercedes congregavit misit eas in saccum
pertusum. Hec dicit dominus exercituum: Ponite
corda vestra super vias vestras. Ascendite in montem,
portate ligna et edificate domum, et accepta
bilis michi erit, et glorificabor, dicit dominus. Re
spexistis ad amplius, et ecce factum est minus;
et intulistis in domum, et exsufflavi illud. Propter
quam ob causam? dicit dominus exercituum. Quia domus
mea deserta est, et vos festinatis unusquisque
in domum suam. Propter hoc super vos prohibiti sunt
celi ne darent rorem, et terra prohibita est ne
daret germen suum. Et vocavi siccitatem
super terram et super montes et super triticum et super
vinum et super oleum et quecumque profert humus,
et super homines et super iumenta et super omnem labo
rem manuum. Et audivit Zorobabel fi
lius Salathiel et Ihesus filius Iosedech sacer
dos magnus et omnes reliquie populi vo
cem domini dei sui et verba Aggei prophete sicut
misit eum dominus deus eorum ad eos, et timu

reduced

in primitiis · et in penuria vos maledicti estis ·
et vos me fraudatis et defigitis gens tota · Infer
te omnem decimam in horreum meum ut sit cibus in do
mo mea · et probate me super hoc dicit dominus · Si non a
peruero vobis cattharactas celi · et effundero vobis
benedictionem usque ad habundantiam · Et increpabo pro
vobis devorantem · et non corrumpet fructum ter
re vestre · nec erit sterilis vinea in agro dicit dominus ex
ercituum · et beatos vos dicent omnes gentes · Eritis enim
vos terra desiderabilis dicit dominus exercituum · Invalu
erunt super me verba vestra dicit dominus · Et dixistis · Quid
locuti contra te sumus · et dixistis · Vanus est qui
servit deo · quod emolumentum quia custodivimus pre
cepta eius · et quia ambulavimus tristes coram
domino exercituum · Ergo nunc beatos dicimus arrogantes
Siquidem edificati sunt facientes impietatem et
temptaverunt deum et salvi facti sunt · Timentes deum tunc
locuti sunt unusquisque cum proximo suo · et atten
dit dominus · et audivit · Et scriptus est liber monumen
ti coram eo timentibus deum · et cogitantibus nomen eius
et erunt michi ait dominus exercituum in die qua ego faciam
in peculium · et parcam eis sicut parcit vir filio suo ser
vienti sibi · Et convertemini et videbitis quid sit
inter iustum et impium · et inter servientem deo et non
servientem ei · IIII

Ecce enim dies veniet succensa quasi caminus ·
Et erunt omnes superbi · et omnes facientes im
pietatem stipula · et inflammabit eos dies veniens
dicit dominus exercituum que non derelinquet eis radicem · et
germen · et orietur vobis timentibus nomen meum sol ius
titie · et sanitas in pennis eius · Et egrediemini et salietis
sicut vituli de armento · et calcabitis impios cum
fuerint cinis sub planta pedum vestrorum in die qua ego
facio dicit dominus exercituum · Mementote legis moysi servi
mei quam mandavi ei in oreb ad omnem israel precepta
et iudicia · Ecce ego mittam vobis heliam prophetam ante
quam veniat dies domini magnus · et horribilis · et con
vertet cor patrum ad filios · et cor filiorum ad patres eorum ne
forte veniam et percutiam terram anathemate · amen ·

Prologus in machabeorum

Domino
excellentissimo et in cultu christi
ane religionis strenuissimo
ludowico regi rabbanus vilis
simus servorum dei in domino dominorum
perpetuam optat salutem · Cum sim promptus animo
ad parendum atque serviendum vestre voluntati co
tidie cogito quid honorificentie vestre gratum exhi
beam · ut mei memoria sedulo apud vos mane
at · et devotio fidelis mee erga obsequium vestrum ap
pareat · Unde grandis mihi quondam incumbit angustia animo
versatur cogitandi quid potissimum reverentie vestre
offeram · quia alii vestre id quod sibi condecet et opu
lentia rerum · vires illis ministrat multipli
ca vobis detulerunt munera · Ego autem ita per me hoc
efficere posse sentio · Sed tamen vacuus a munere pe
nitus non ero · quia vestre parvitatem virium mearum et in
genii tenuitatem ea que in meditatione sanctarum scriptu
rarum elaboravi offerre decerno · que licet non sint con
digna prudentie vestre · tamen credo non sunt ubique
spernenda · Preterito siquidem anno transmisi vobis trac
tatum in danielem prophetam · qui non solum ex dictis
maiorum · quin etiam ex nostre parvitatis sensu conferam ·
fluunt ideo quia tempus est illud quo romana ecclesia
eorumdem librorum expositionem · quam ante annos
aliquot rogantibus amicis sensu hystorico simul
et allegorico dictaveram excellentie vestre deferro in
si aliquem sensum misticum in eis dinoscere vos dele
ctet habeatis in promptu quod illum explicitum inveni
re valeatis · non dico valde diserte · et orationem re
thorica · sed lucido sermone et catholica fide · Vos
quorum siquid in predicto opere repperitis vobis gratum
et vestre placitum eius gratie · hoc deputetis · a quo est omne
bonum · Siquid autem minus recte vel inconvenienter
positum vobis ibidem videatur · imperitie mee m
magis deputetis quam malitie · qui quamdiu in hoc
corpusculo vivero · in christi servitio pro mee possibili
tatis sum laborare contendo · Apostolus enim est mihi te
qui michi in animo hoc dedit velle ipsum me bono ope
faciat consummare de quo propheta ait · Prope est dominus
invocantibus se in veritate · et non derelinquet omnes
sperantes in se · Divinitas domini nostri ihesu christi diu
vos hic incolumes · et legis dei veritate manen
tes ad multorum salutem custodiat · et post huius vite
cursum ad vitam eternam beatitudinis pervenire
concedat ·

Secundus prologus machabeorum

Reverentissimo et omni caritatis
officio dignissimo geroldo sa
cri palacii archidiachonus
rabanus vilis dei servus
servorum in christo salutem · Men
ini me in palatio vvangi
onum civitatis constitutum tecum habere sermonem
de eminentia sanctarum scripturarum · et de difficultate di
vinarum hystoriarum in quibus non solum pro aliquanta lo
ca propter varietatem rerum et situum · perimitiarum obs
curius est sensus · quam etiam per tropos figurarum obscurior
est intellectus · et quia eodem tempore commentarios in li
bros regum nuper a nobis editos venerabili abbati
constituit libros machabeorum legi in ecclesia

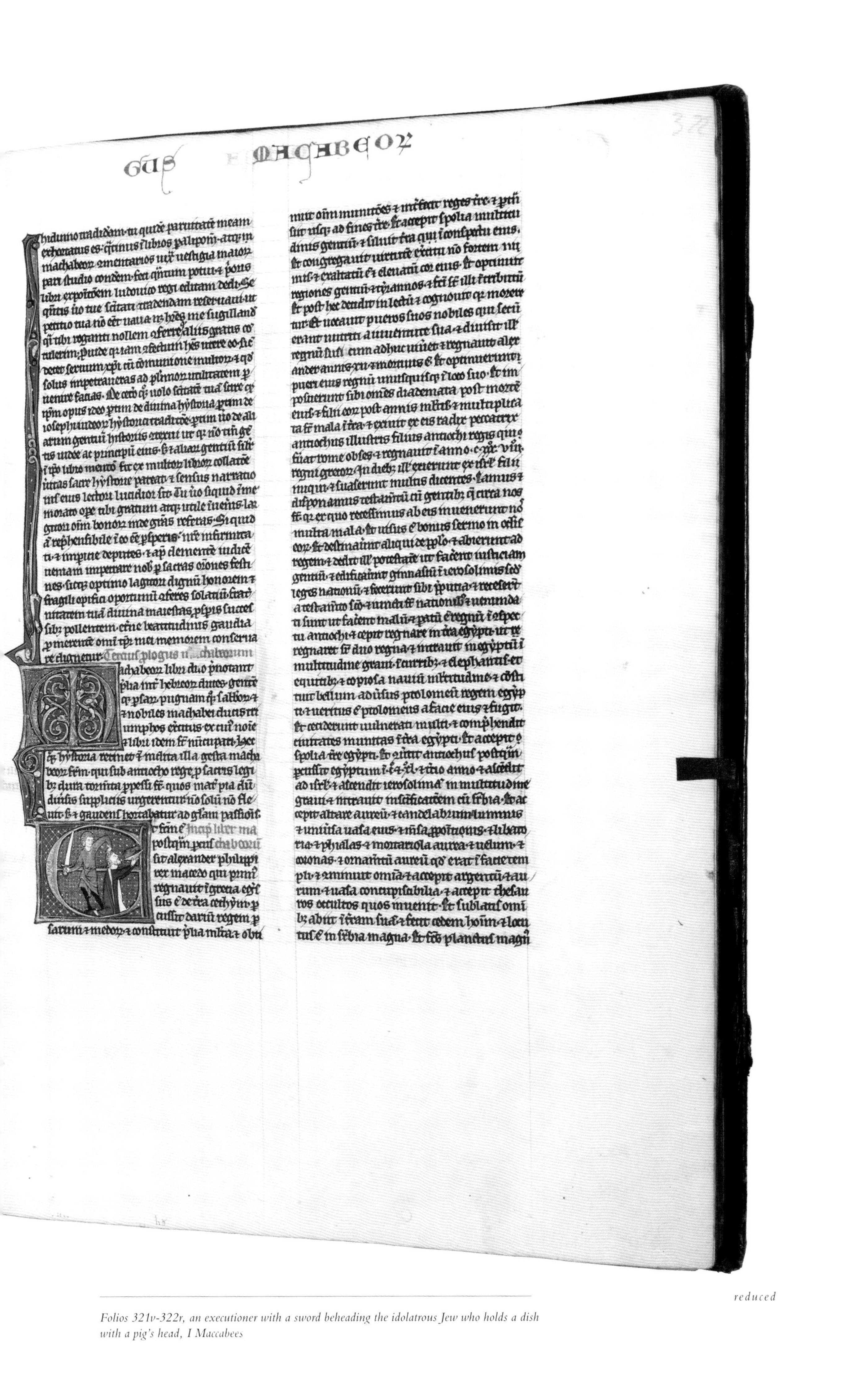

reduced

Folios 321v-322r, an executioner with a sword beheading the idolatrous Jew who holds a dish with a pig's head, I Maccabees

52. An executioner with a sword beheading the idolatrous Jew who holds a dish with a pig's head, 7 lines, 30 x 42 mm., folio 322r, I Maccabees.

53. A Jew of Jerusalem giving a letter to a kneeling boy to take to Egypt, 7 lines, 31 x 33 mm., with extension to 260 mm. high, folio 334v, II Maccabees.

54. Jesse asleep, with a tree growing from his loins including the Virgin Mary and Christ in its branches, 6 lines with indented ascender bringing the height to 16 lines, 72 x 32 mm., with extension to 92 mm. high, folio 340r, Matthew.

55. Saint Mark standing in a church, his bull below, 24 lines (an initial 'I'), 110 x 15 mm., with extension to 247 mm. high, folio 350v, Mark.

56. Zechariah waving a censer over an altar, God above, 7 lines with indented descender bringing the height to 31 lines, 33 x 33 mm., with extension to 232 mm. high, folio 357v, Luke.

57. Saint John standing in a church, his eagle below, 40 lines (an initial 'I'), 180 x 14 mm., with extension to 268 mm. high, folio 369r, John.

58. Saint Paul holding a cross and preaching towards a group of Jews, 6 lines with indented descender bringing the height to 16 lines, 27 x 33 mm., with extension to 206 mm. high, folio 378r, Romans.

59. A bishop holding a letter and giving communion to a kneeling couple, (I Corinthians 7), 8 lines with indented descender bringing the height to 30 lines, 36 x 37 mm., with extension to 237 mm., folio 382v, I Corinthians.

60. An angel visiting Saint Paul in bed, 5 lines (at foot of page, extending into lower margin), 30 x 30 mm., with extension to 287 mm. high, folio 386v, II Corinthians.

61. Saint Paul propelling a man forward by the shoulder, while the man pushes the woman, 6 lines with indented descender bringing the height to 25 lines, 27 x 32 mm., with extension to 150 mm. high, folio 389v, Galatians.

62. A soldier guarding Saint Paul in prison (alluding to Ephesians 3:1), 5 lines with indented descender bringing the height to 8 lines, 23 x 28 mm., with extension to 227 mm., folio 390v, Ephesians.

63. Saint Paul witnessing the beheading of a young boy (perhaps a reference to Paul as Saul persecuting the church, Philippians 3:6), 7 lines with indented descender bringing the height to 21 lines, 34 x 29 mm., with extension to 257 mm. high, folio 392r, Philippians.

64. Saint Paul talking to a horned Moses, who is breaking the tablets of the Law (perhaps alluding to the Jewish laws being no longer relevant, Colossians 3:11), 6 lines with indented descender bringing the height to 14 lines, 27 x 32 mm., with extension to 268 mm. high, folio 393r, Colossians.

65. Saul witnessing the defeat of the son of perdition, shown as a king, 6 lines with indented descender bringing the height to 24 lines, 28 x 29 mm., with extension to 180 mm., folio 395r, Thessalonians.

66. Saint Paul (or a Bishop) invests a priest with a chasuble (probably in reference to I Timothy 3 on the role of bishops and deacons), 7 lines with indented descender bringing the height to 22 lines, 32 x 30 mm., with extension to 225 mm., folio 395v, I Timothy.

67. Saint Paul crowning a warrior, or blessing a warrior's crown, 4 lines with indented descender bringing the height to 12 lines, 19 x 27 mm., with extension to 268 mm., folio 396v, II Timothy.

68. A seated king thrashing a boy stripped to the waist, watched by another man (perhaps referring to the punishment of rebellious people,Titus 1:13), 6 lines with indented descender bringing the height to 23 lines, 28 x 32 mm., with extension to 240 mm., folio 398v,Titus.

69. The Ascension, the Apostles and the Virgin Mary watching as Christ's feet disappear upwards, 6 lines with indented descender bringing the height to 34 lines, 27 x 30 mm., with extension to 260 mm., folio 401v, Acts.

70. Saint James holding a book and standing in a church, 24 lines (an initial 'I'), 110 x 15 mm., with extension to 240 mm. high, folio 413r, James.

71. Saint Peter dressed as a bishop holding keys, 6 lines with indented descender bringing the height to 28 lines, 28 x 28 mm., with extension to 257 mm. high, folio 414r, I Peter.

72. Saint Peter dressed as a priest with a very large key, 7 lines, 31 x 35 mm., with extension to 152 mm., folio 415v, II Peter.

73. Saint John standing, 7 lines, 32 x 33 mm., with extension to 228 mm. high, folio 416r, I John.

74. Saint John standing with a book, 6 lines, 27 x 32 mm., with extension to 220 mm. high, folio 417r, II John.

75. Saint John standing, 6 lines, 27 x 32 mm., with extension to 140 mm. high, folio 417v, III John.

76. Jude standing on a pedestal, 10 lines (an initial 'I'), 51 x 17 mm., with extension to 135 mm. high, also folio 417v, Jude.

77. Saint John writing with the churches of Asia behind him, 6 lines, 29 x 31 mm., with extension to 280 mm. high, folio 418r, Revelation.

The manuscript is also richly ornamented with decorated initials, principally for prologues and other major divisions, all with long extensions far into the margins and often including dragons and other pictorial ornament. They are: 1, 8-line (replaced), folio 32r; 2, 5-line, folio 66v; 3, 7-line, folio 85r; 4, 6-line, folio 129v; 5, 5-line, folio 139r; 6, 7-line, folio 151v; 7, 6-line, folio 163r; 8, 6-line, folio 168v; 9, 4-line, folio 173r; 10, 6-line, folio 177v; 11, 4-line, also folio 177v; 12, 49 lines (an initial 'I' the full height of the page), including three grotesques with human heads, one playing a pipe, folio 208r; 13, 5-line, including two hooded heads, folio 215r; 14, 4-line but with ascender extending it to 19 lines, folio 219r; 15, 6-line, folio 224v; 16, 7-line, folio 239r; 17, 26 lines (an initial 'I'), including two grotesques with human heads, one with an axe, folio 256r; 18, 3-line but with ascender extending it to 10 lines, folio 277v; 19, initial 'I' running up the margin, folio 279r; 20, 8-line, extension including a long-legged bird, perhaps an ostrich, folio 280r; 21, 8-line, folio 297v; 22, 4-line, folio 306v; 23, 5-line, folio 308v; 24, 17 lines (an initial 'I'), folio 310r; 25, 5-line, also folio 310r; 26, 3-line, folio 310v; 27, 14 lines (an initial 'I'), including a blue lion standing on its hind legs, also folio 310v; 28, 4-line, supporting an ostrich, folio 311r; 29, 4-line, also folio 311r; 30, 5-line, folio 312v; 31, 6-line, including a large orange dog in the undergrowth, folio 314r; 32, 5-line, folio 314v; 33, 4-line, folio 315r; 34, 5-line, folio

sed in mentem habere adiutoria sibi facta de celo et
nunc sperarent ab omnipotente sibi affuturam vic
toriam. Et allocutus est eos de lege et prophetis admo
nens et certamina que fecerant prius promptiores
eos constituit et ita animis eorum erectis simul osten
dens gentium fallaciam et iuramentorum prevaricati
onem. Singulos autem illorum armavit non clipei et
haste munitione sed sermonibus optimis et horta
tionibus exposito digno fide somnio per quod univer
sos letificavit. Erat autem huiusmodi visus. Oniam qui fue
rat summus sacerdos virum bonum et benignum vere
cundum visu modestum moribus et eloquio decorum et
qui a puero in virtutibus exercitatus sit manus pro
tendentem orare pro populo iudeorum. Post hec appa
ruisse et alium virum etate et gloria mirabilem il
lum. Respondentem vero Oniam dixisse: Hic est
fratrum amator et populi israel: hic est qui multum orat pro
populo et universa sancta civitate Ieremias propheta dei. Exten
disse autem Ieremiam dexteram et dedisse iude gladi
um aureum dicentem: Accipe sanctum gladium mu
nus a deo quo deicies adversarios populi mei israel. Ex
hortati itaque iude de quibus extolli posset impetus et
animi iuvenum confortari statuerunt dimica
re et confligere fortiter ut virtus de negociis iudi
caret eo quod civitas sancta et templum periclitarentur.
Erat enim pro uxoribus et filiis itemque pro fratribus et cogna
tis minor sollicitudo. Maximus vero et primus
pro sanctitate timor erat templi. Sed et eos qui in civita
te erant non minima sollicitudo habebat pro hiis qui
congressuri erant. Et iam cum omnes sperarent iu
dicium futurum hostesque adessent atque exercitus erat
ordinatus. bestie equitesque oportuno in loco com
positi. considerans machabeus adventum multi
tudinis et apparatum varium armorum ac ferocita
tem bestiarum extendens manus in celum prodi
gia facientem dominum invocavit qui non secundum ar
morum potentiam sed prout ipsi placet dat dignis
victoriam. Dixit autem invocans hoc modo. Tu domine qui
misisti angelum tuum sub ezechiam rege iude
et interfecisti de castris sennacherib .c.lxxxv. milia. Et nunc
dominator celorum mitte angelum tuum bonum ante nos
in timore et tremore magnitudinis brachii tui
ut metuant qui cum blasphemia veniunt contra
adversus sanctum populum tuum. Et hic quidem ita peroravit.
Nichanor autem et qui cum eo erant cum tubis et can
ticis admovebant. Iudas vero et qui cum eo erant
invocato deo per orationes congressi
sunt. manu quidem pugnantes. sed dominum cordi
bus orantes prostraverunt non minus .xxxv. milia presen

et magni decoris habitudine circa || et moib; tois valde

tia dei magnifice delectati. Cumque cessassent et
cum gaudio redirent: cognoverunt nichanorem
ruisse cum armis suis. Facto itaque clamore et pertur
batione excitata patria voce omnipotentem dominum
benedicebant. Precepit autem iudas qui per omnia corpo
re et animo mori pro civibus paratus erat: caput nicha
noris et manum cum humero abscisam ierosolimam
perferri. Quo cum pervenisset: convocatis contri
bulibus et sacerdotibus ad altare accersiit et eos qui
in arce erant. Et ostenso capite nichanoris et ma
nu nefaria quam extendens contra domum sanctam omni
potentis dei magnifice gloriatus est linguam etiam
impii nichanoris precisam iussit particulatim a
vibus dari. manum autem dementis contra templum sus
pendi. Omnes igitur benedixerunt dominum celi dicen
tes. Benedictus qui locum suum incontaminatum conserva
vit. Suspendit autem nichanoris caput in summa ar
ce evidens ut esset et manifestum signum auxilii
dei. Itaque omnes communi consilio decreverunt nullo mo
do diem istum absque celebritate preterire. habere autem cele
britatem tertia decima die mensis adar qui dicitur vo
ce syriaca pridie mardochei die. Igitur hiis erga ni
chanorem gestis. et ex illis temporibus ab hebreis civi
tate possessa. ego quoque in hiis faciam finem
sermonis. Et siquidem bene et ut historie compe
tit et hoc ipse velim. Si autem minus digne conceden
dum est michi. Sicut enim vinum semper bibere aut
semper aquam contrarium est alternis autem uti delecta
bile. ita legentibus si semper exactus sit sermo:
non erit gratus. Hic ergo erit consummatus.

Prologus Mathei evangeliste

Matheus ex iudea sicut primus
in ordine ponitur. ita evan
gelium in iudea primus scrip
sit. cuius vocatio ad deum ex
publicanis actibus fuit duo
rum in generatione christi principia
presumens unius cuiusque prima circumcisio
in carne alterius cuius secundum cor electio fuit. Et ex utris
que enim patribus christus. sicque quaternario numero tri
formiter posito principium a credendi fide in elec
tionis tempus porrigens et electione usque in transmi
grationis diem dirigens atque a transmigrationis
die usque in christum diffiniens decursam adventus
domini ostendit generationem et numero satisfaciens
et tempori ut et se quid esset ostenderet et dei in se opus de
monstrans et in hiis quorum genus posuit christi o
perantis a principio testimonium non negaret.
Quarum omnium rerum tempus ordo numerus dispositio vel

reduced

Folios 339v-340r, Jesse asleep, with a tree growing from his loins including the Virgin Mary and Christ in its branches, Matthew

se in carne. hic e seductor & antixpc. Videte uos
met ipos ne pdatis q operati estis. s; ut mercede
plena accipiatis. Omes qui recedunt & no per
manent in doctrina xpi dm no hnt. Qui p
manet i doctrina hic & prem & filium ht. Si
quis uenit ad uos & hanc doctrinam no fert
nolite eum recipe i domu nec aue ei dixeritis.
Qui dicit illi aue comicat opibz eius malignis
Ecce pdixi uobis ut no i die dni confundamini. Pl
plura hns uobis scribere nolui p cartam & attram
tum. Spero enim futurum me ad uos & os ad os lo
qui ut gaudium urm sit plenum. Salutant te fi
lii sororis tue electe. Gra tecum. am. Alia epla

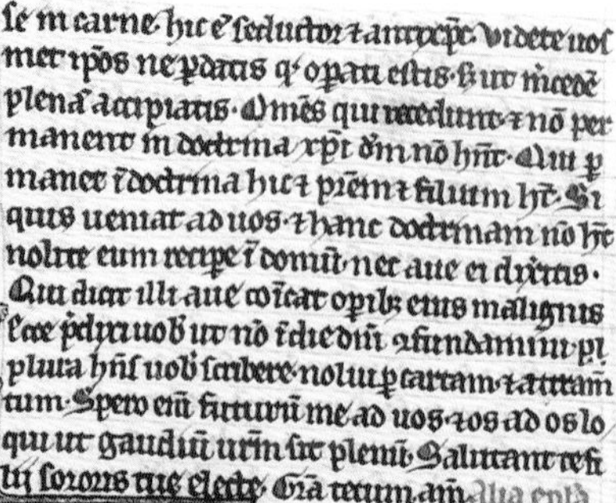

enior Gaio iohannis tercia
kmo que ego diligo i ueritate
caritatis kme in omibz ora
nem facio, pspe te ingredi &
ualere sic pspe agit aia tua
Gauisus sum ualde uenie
tibz fribz & testimonium phibentibz ueritati tue sic
tu in ueritate ambulas. Maiorem horu no hbeo g
ciam q ut audiam filios meos i ueritate ambulare
kme fideliter facis quicquid operaris in fres & p
hoc in pegrinos qui testimonium ecce reddiderunt
caritati tue in conspectu eccle quos bn faciens de
duces digne deo. P noie enim pfecti sunt nich ac
cipientes a gentilibz. Nos g debemus suscipe hui
modi. ut cooperatores simus ueritatis. Scripsissem
forsitan eccle. s; is qui amat primatum gerere
in eis diotrepes no recipit nos. Pp hoc si uenero
commoueam eius opa que facit uerbis maligni
nis garriens i nos & qsi ista no ei sufficiant
neq; ipe suscepit fres & eos qui suscipiunt phi
bet & de eccla eicit. kme noli imitari malum. s;
qd bonum e. Qui bn facit ex deo e. Qui aut ma
lefacit no uidet dm. Demetrio testimonium red
ditur ab hoibz & ab ipa ueritate. S; & nos testim
onium phibemus & nosti qm testimonium nrm
uerum e. Multa hui tibi scribere s; nolui per
attramentum & calamum scribere. Spero aut
ptinus te uidere & os ad os loquemur.
pax tibi. Salutant te amici. Saluta
tu amicos nominatim. Incipit epi
udas ihu xpi seruus stola iude
fr iacobi hiis qui in deo patre dilectis & i
xpo ihu conseruatis & uocatis. Mia uobis
& pax & caritas adimpleatur. kmi oem
sollicitudinem faciens scribendi uobis de coi
ura salute necce hui scribere uobis depre

cans supcertari semel tradite fidei sce
ierunt enim quidam homines impii qui
scripti sunt in hoc iudicium dei nri gra
ferentes in luxuriam & solum dnator
dnm nrm ihm xpm negantes. Com
uos uolo scientes semel omia qm ihc
tra egypti saluans. Scdo eos qui no cr
pdidit. Anglos uo qui no seruauerunt
tum suum. s; dereliquerunt suum domicil
iudicium magni dei uinclis eternis sb
reseruauit. Sic sodoma & gomorra &
ciuitates simili modo exfornicate abe
carnem alteram fce st exemplum igni
penam sustinentes. Similiter et hi
carnem maculant dnatoem aut s
i maiestatem blasphemant. Cum m
archangelus cum diabolo disputans
tur de moysi corpore n e ausus iudicium
ei blasphemie. s; dixit. Imperet tibi dns
Qcumq; quidem ignorant blasphem
Quecumq; aut naturaliter tamqm muta
nouerunt in his corrumpuntur. Ve illi
uia caym abierunt & errore balaam
effusi sunt & in contradictoe chore peri
hii sunt in eplis suis macle conuiuan
timore semet ipos pascentes nubes si
a uentis circumferuntur arbores au
nales infructuose bis mortue eradica
tus feri maris despumantes suas co
Sydera errantia quibz pcella tenebrar
seruata e in eternum. Pphetauit aut de
timus ab adam enoch dicens. Ecce
dns in scis milibz suis facere iudiciu
omnes & arguere omes impios de o
pibz impietatis eorum quibz impie eger
omnibz duris que locuti st contra dm
impii. Hii sunt murmuratores q
desideria ambulantes & os illorum lo
superbiam mirantes psonas questus c
aut kmi memores estote ubor q p
uobis aplis dni nri ihu xpi qui dic
uobis qm in nouissimis temporibz
illusores scdm desideria sua ambu
non i pietate. Hii st qui segregant s
animales spm no hntes. Vos kmi s
tes uosmet ipos in dilcoe dei scissi
fidei in spu orantes uosmet ipos in
dei seruantes expectantes miam
ihu xpi in uitam eternam & hos qu

reduced

Folios 417v-418r, Jude standing on a pedestal, Jude; Saint John writing with the churches of Asia behind him, Revelation

316r; 35, 19 lines (an initial 'I') including a grotesque in a yellow top, folio 317r; 36, 5-line, folio 317v; 37, 5-line, folio 320v; 38, 5-line, folio 321v; 39, 6-line, also folio 321v; 40, 6-line, folio 322r; 41, 7-line, folio 339v; 42, 6-line, folio 340r; 43, 7-line, including two battling grotesques, folio 350v; 44, 8-line, including a grotesque centaur with bow and arrow, folio 357v; 45, 4-line but with ascender extending it to 8 lines, also folio 357v; 46, 6-line but with ascender extending it to 17 lines, folio 369r; 47, 4-line, folio 377v; 48, 8-line, also folio 377v; 49, 5-line, folio 382r; 50, 4-line, folio 386v; 51, 5-line, folio 389v; 52, 2-line, folio 390v; 53, 6-line, folio 393r; 54, 4-line, folio 393r; 55, 3-line, folio 395r; 56, 2-line enclosing a black bird, folio 395v; 57, initial 'I' running up the margin, folio 396v; 58, 2-line, folio 398v; 59, 3-line, folio 401v; 60, 4-line, folio 413r; 61, 6-line with a crane standing on top, folio 418r; 62, 6-line, folio 424r; 63, 4-line, folio 430r; 64, 5-line, folio 433r; 65, 5-line, folio 435r; 66, 5-line, folio 438r; 67, 4-line, folio 439r; 68, 5-line with indented ascender extending it to 12 lines, folio 440r; 69, 10-line (initial 'I'), folio 442r; 70, 5-line with indented ascender extending it to 13 lines, folio 444r; 71, 6-line, folio 444v; 72, 6-line, folio 447r; 73, 6-line, folio 448r; 74, 5-line with indented descender extending it to 19 lines, folio 449r; 75, 6-line, folio 449v; 76, 6-line, folio 450v; 77, 6-line, folio 454v; 78, 6-line, folio 456v; and 79, 3-line, also folio 456v.

PROVENANCE

1. Written and illuminated in Paris, the cultural capital of Europe by the late thirteenth century, the seat of the royal court, the cathedral of Notre Dame and the largest university in the world. There is a contemporary note by a stationer in a minute hand at the foot of the last leaf, "xxxix pieces" (actually there are 38 gatherings, but maybe the counting included the flyleaves). The *secundo folio*, which might eventually permit identification of the Bible in a medieval inventory, is "Neque enim." There is a long erasure below the end of the text, which may yet be scientifically recoverable.

2. Like a number of thirteenth-century Bibles, the manuscript was brought back on the market in the early fifteenth century, at a time when large Latin Bibles were once again becoming fashionable. A fine illuminated border was added to the first leaf in the Parisian style of about 1420, and (to judge from offsets) a similar border once surrounded the Genesis page.

3. Later still, for it covers some of the decoration, a coat-of-arms was added at the foot of folio 1r, probably in the fifteenth century, party per fess *gules* and *sable*, overall a lion *or*. No arms with exactly these charges are recorded by T. de Renesse, *Dictionnaire de figures héraldiques*, VI, 1902, p. 247. They are probably Italian. Some of the late medieval notes, including some chapter numbering, may be in an Italian hand; the gothic trefoil fittings in the cover look Italian.

4. Lucien Delamarre; his sale, Théophile Belin, Paris, 8 May 1909, lot 3.

5. From the same private collection as the *Romance of Troy*, below.

PUBLISHED REFERENCES

As far as we are aware, the manuscript has not been published or mentioned since the Delamarre sale of 1909.

FURTHER LITERATURE

For traditional thirteenth-century Latin Bibles, see:
DE HAMEL, C. *The Book, A History of the Bible*, London, 2001, chapter 5, pp. 114-39.
ELEEN, L. *The Illustration of the Pauline Epistles in French and English Bibles of the Twelfth and Thirteenth Centuries*, Oxford and New York, 1982.
LIGHT, L. "The Thirteenth Century and the Paris Bible," in R. Marsden and E.A. Matter, eds., *The New Cambridge History of the Bible*, II, Cambridge, 2012, pp. 380-91.
RUZZIER, C. "The Miniaturisation of Bible Manuscripts in the Thirteenth Century, A Comparative Study," in E. Poleg and L. Light, eds., *Form and Function in the Late Medieval Bible*, Leiden, 2013, pp. 105-25.

For the Psalter of Saint Louis, see:
BRANNER, R. *Manuscript Painting in Paris during the Reign of Saint Louis, A Study of Styles*, Berkeley and Los Angeles, 1977, esp. pp. 132-37.
STONES, A. *Gothic Manuscripts, 1260-1320*, I, ii, *Catalogue* (Survey of Manuscripts Illuminated in France 3), London and Turnhout, 2013, cat. 1-11, pp. 20-23.
THOMAS, M. *Le Psautier de Saint Louis*, facsimile (Codices Selecti 37), Graz, 1985.

ONLINE RESOURCES

Stegmüller, Repertorium biblicum medii aevi (digital edition)
http://repbib.uni-trier.de/cgi-bin/rebihome.tcl

se in carne hic e seductor z anticristus. videte uos
ne pdatis que operati estis. Sz ut mcede
plena accipiatis. Omnis qui recedit z no ht i
manento in doctrina xpi dm non ht. Qui
manet in doctrina hic z patrem z filium
quis uenit ad uos z hanc doctrinam non
affert nolite recipere eum in domum nec aue ei dix
eritis. Qui enim dicit illi aue comunicat operib eius mal
is. Plura habens uobis scribere nolui p cartam
z atramentum. Spero enim futurum me ad uos z
os ad os loqui ut gaudium urm sit plenum. Salu
tant te filii sororis tue electe. Gra tecum.

Senior gaio ca
rissimo que ego
diligo in ueritate.
Caris
sime de omnibz ora
tionem facio prospe
re te ingredi z uale
re sicut prospere agit
anima tua. Gauisus
sum ualde uenienti

bus fribz z testimonium perhibenti
bus ueritati tue sicut tu in ueritate ambula
s. Maiorem horum non habeo gratiam ut audiam filios
meos in ueritate ambulare. Carissime fideliter facis
quicquid operaris in fratres z hoc in peregrinos
qui testimonium reddiderunt caritati tue in conspectu
ecclesie quos benefaciens deduces digne
deo. Pro nomine enim profecti sunt nichil accipientes a g
entibus. Nos ergo debemus suscipere huiusmodi ut coo
peratores simus ueritatis. Scripsissem forsitan eccle
sie sed is qui amat primatum gerere in eis
diotrephes non recipit nos. Propter hoc si uenero como
nebo eius opera que facit uerbis malignis
garriens in nos z quasi non ei ista sufficiant nec ipse

de tiuce auoit par my le corps
vn confenone a tout le fer et le
bruit couppee entrauers et en sen
tiente ? pale com celui qui la
sentoit sa mort si com il pot
parler si dit a Achilles Cuert
bien adroit pouez de traison estre
appellez qui nous esgardez a
ocire par les mains de nos
ennemis et direz que tous so
mes desconfis ne oncques les

THE ROMANCE OF TROY

THE ROMANCE OF TROY

In French prose, illuminated manuscript on parchment
Southern Netherlands, probably Brussels, c. 1450-1460
17 large miniatures by the Master of Girart de Roussillon and Workshop

This is the finest and most richly illuminated extant manuscript of the version called "Prose 1" of the Romance of Troy, which is the earliest great rendering of the Trojan legend in the French language. Its miniatures are by the artist known as the Master of Girart de Roussillon, named after the manuscript in Vienna of the Roman de Girart de Roussillon. Probably identical with Dreux Jean, this rare and accomplished illuminator worked for the court of the dukes of Burgundy, and this manuscript must also come from the ducal circle. The addition of a newly attributed manuscript to the elusive and incomparable Master himself is a major event in the scholarship of southern Netherlandish art. This is probably the finest manuscript of Trojan romance ever likely to be sold again.

Previous page: Folios 69v-70r, Achilles and Ajax playing chess in a tent, as Trojan knights in gold and silver armor remonstrate at their idleness

Facing page: Folio 18v, Menelaus, jilted husband of Helen, in conversation with his brother Agamemnon, meeting on horseback in a landscape attended by other Greek noblemen

ton aieul ninus quant tu verras
tes enffans occire et ta ville
destruire et toy mesmes en mor:
ras autant dou seul honteusement

The romance of the siege and destruction of Troy and the diaspora of the Trojans is the greatest literary text of Antiquity, both in Greek and Latin. It became the supreme aspiration of the Middle Ages to claim descent from the chivalric knights of Troy. The origins of Rome were traced to Aeneas; Britain was reputedly so-called after Brutus of Troy; Paris was named after the Trojan prince whose abduction of Helen led to the war; and Troyes was to be the new Troy. The first printed book in the English language was a Trojan romance (c. 1474). Above all, the fifteenth-century Dukes of Burgundy reveled in their supposed descent from the Trojans and they promoted it unceasingly. The library of Philip the Good, duke of Burgundy 1419-1467, included seventeen manuscripts on the history of Troy, and at least ten copies were owned by his successors Charles the Bold (1467-1477) and Philip the Handsome (1482-1506) (A. Bayot, *La légende de Troie à la cour de Bourgogne*, Bruges, 1908; J. Barrois, *Bibliothèque Prototypographique*, Paris, 1830, pp. 143-45 and 239-41). Since the artist of the present manuscript was a full-time employee of Charles the Bold (see below), it is by no means impossible that this manuscript too was destined for the ducal library. At the very least, it is the finest surviving manuscript of a text consciously promoted from within the Burgundian court.

Jean Wauquelin Presenting his *Chroniques de Hainaut* to Philip the Good, *Chroniques de Hainaut*, frontispiece illuminated by Rogier van der Weyden, c. 1447-1448 (Brussels, Bibliothèque royale de Belgique, MS 9242, fol. 1r)

Folio 1r, Philosophers instructing a king, perhaps King Laomedon, who is seated below a canopy in a gothic throne room

Ci commence li prologue de la
vraie hystoire de Troye

Li anciens sages que de phi
losophie eurent mestier nous
deffendent a mener nostre vie
oiseusement et sans labour et pource q
oiseuse esmuet et encline le corps a de
lices. Et pour ce amerent ilz gaster
et travailler leurs corps non tant seu
lement a leur propre prouffit mais
au comun bien de tous les autres.
Car si come li repos est racine des
vices multiplier et daccroistre aussi
est labour et travail nourrissement
et accroissance de nettoyer. Et pour
ce devons nous bien mettre nostre
cueur en deffendre les euvres des
anciens et des vieilles histoires

Car en elles puet len assez apren
dre des biens et des maulx qui se
avienent en leurs affaires et tout
ce nous est necessaire chose a savoir
Ce est le bien pour ouvrer par nous
et par noz amis et le mal pour es
chiver quant aucune chose puet
sourvenir que ticuer nous dye
Car par les choses passees puet
len moult miex de celles qui sont
avenir et se puet moult aidier en
recouvrer la deffaulte que Aristo
tes dit que est es jennes homes
la ou il dit que jennes home ne
puet estre ce par esprouve de viel
les choses et de grant esprouve ne
puet estre si tres longuement et nous
devons savoir que li philosophes
entendirent en deux manieres ce
est que muet deritage par usage et
qui sapartment nostre parage et il est
miex par nobles cuers et par
honneste vie et telz jenne fait plus
a loer que li vieillart qui maine sa
vie dissoluement. Car aussi honne
ste et la bonne maniere que li jen
nes home par sa bonne nature et
par usage la remembrance des viel
les hystoires et des grant ouvrres
et li bons exemples doubtent la
jennesse et eslievent et adrecent
li courage a vigoreusement valoir
et ouvrer euvres de vertus a ce q
leur vie de chemin est bonne naturel

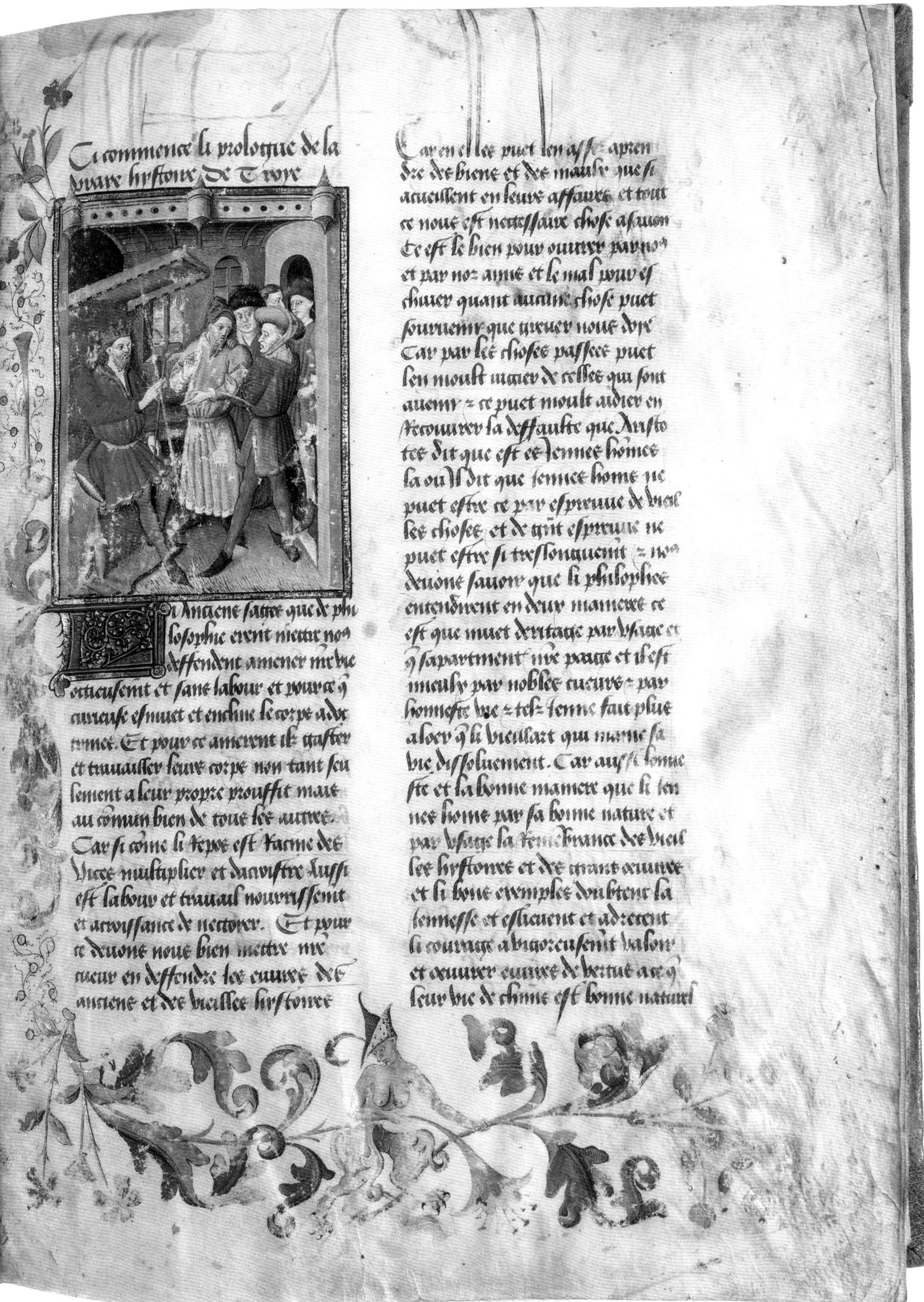

reduced

leure Mais sur toute chose amerott
elle le mariage. Comment me
dea ama Jason et le mist a
raison.

Ainsi souffri medea toute une
sepmaine ceste prime damo[ur]
et moult pensoit curieusement en
quel maniere elle peust avoir son

The earliest great working of the Trojan legend in the French language was the twelfth-century *Roman de Troie* of Benoît de Sainte-Maure, in just over 30,000 lines of epic verse. In the thirteenth century, this poem was rendered for the first time into French prose, perhaps to add credibility to what might have been dismissed as fiction when chivalric romance became paramount during the Crusades. That original version, known to literary historians as "Prose 1," is the text represented by the manuscript here. The author claims to have written it in the Morea, now the Peloponnese peninsula, then a Frankish principality. It opens with a description of the geography of the eastern Mediterranean, followed by the legend of Jason and the Golden Fleece which resulted in the first destruction of Troy, the romance itself from Benoît de Sainte-Maure through to the return and death of Ulysses, and finally a short continuation taken from the romance of Landomata, son of Hector, who returned to Troy and re-established a knightly kingdom. All these are characteristic of the "Prose 1" version.

The most up-to-date and detailed list of surviving manuscripts of "Prose 1" is that on the website of ARLIMA, Archives de littérature du Moyen Âge, recording twelve manuscripts of this text, including the present copy, listed as "localisation actuelle inconnue" ("present location unknown"). One of the twelve was destroyed in the Second World War. In approximate order of date, these manuscripts are:

1. Paris, Bibliothèque nationale de France, MS fr. 1612, late thirteenth century, 25 historiated initials.
2. Paris, Bibliothèque nationale de France, MS fr.1627, early fourteenth century, one miniature (very rubbed).
3. Formerly Tours, Bibliothèque municipale, MS 954, dated 1358, on paper, no miniatures; destroyed 19 June 1940.
4. Florence, Biblioteca Riccardiana, cod. 2025, probably fourteenth century, some sketches for miniatures never completed.
5. Maredsous, Bibliothèque de l'Abbaye, MS f° 26, mid-fifteenth century, on paper, 67 colored drawings.
6. The present manuscript, on parchment, 17 illuminated miniatures (with another now in the National Gallery of Art, Washington, see below).
7. Aberystwyth, National Library of Wales, MS 5008, fifteenth century, on paper, incomplete, no miniatures.
8. Lyon, Bibliothèque municipale, MS 878, fifteenth century, incomplete, two miniatures remaining (all others removed).
9. Paris, Bibliothèque nationale de France, MS nouv. acq. fr. 10052, late fifteenth century, on paper, no miniatures.
10. Paris, Bibliothèque nationale de France, MS nouv. acq. fr. 11674, late fifteenth century, on paper, space left for one miniature never added.

Folio 4v, Medea the sorceress, daughter of King Aeëtes, seated on a bench in a gothic room in conversation with Jason, with whom she falls in love, attended by an armed knight, detail

la chose que je plus ayme. puis
li baille un estrupt et li dist mai
tenant que tu verras le mouton
garde que tu ne voies avant iusq
a tant que tu ne sauras dit iii.
foiz contre orient Car par aven
ture les dieux sen courrouceroiet
de ce que tu veulz faire. et po.
ce les repaieras. Ore te baille
iay ceste glus qui est par tel
maniere destrempee que ia ne
la touscheras sitiens que iamais
soit defermee. pour ce ten vas
moult tost vers le beuf et si la
formeras a la bouche et au nez et
maintenant sauront estoupees
et puis leur feras arer quatre
roes. puis yras tout droit au
serpent que grant bataille te
rendra. Mais de ce ne te couuiet
a doubter que tost en seras de
liures et maintenant que tu
lauras conquis oste lui trestouz
les dens et les seme a la terre q
tu auras aree Car ainsi li cou
uient estre et de ce verras tu
maintenant nastre deux chies
armes de toutes armes et deuat
toy se combatront tant que ilz
y seront mors. Adoncques auras
tu tout acheuee ta besoingne.
Mais bien te garde que pour la
victoire que tu auras eue tu ne
soyes oubliez de rendre graces

adieux. Et puis ten yras vers
mouton bellement si en prendr
la toison et lui laisseras et ten
tout maintenant si tar ore to
dit si que je ne te puis plus m
strer. garde que de riens nen so
oubliez et desormais te met al
voie Car il est grant iour ce n
aur. Que si voy cestes amo
sta Jason ..

Jason la prist adonc entre
bras et la mercie mile foi
sen retourne a son lit o tout ce
le li a donne si estoit mlt liez
grant maniere. et pour le beu
que il auoit la nuit fait sen d
maintenant et quant il ot v
po repose si sesueilla et appare
maintenant. Car temps lui s
bloit daler. Mais ses compaig
ont de lui moult grant doubt
quant li roy Oestes voit ce qu
Jason vouloit faire si lui prist
adire moult bonnement. Jaso
fait il de ta mort ne vueil je e
blasmez. Et pour ce te di que se
conseil voulsisse croire tu mv
en nulle maniere Car je noy onc
que nulz y alast que iamais
reuinst arriere Car li dieux ro
muss gardes. Pour quoi je croi
bien que tu vas a ta fin mais s
chees ta force ne te defendrait
Car villenie me sembleroit.

ence que tu vouldras. Mais ce est
contre ma voulente. Que Jason ne
voust entendre la monestement le roy
De chose que li roy dist na cure
Jason riens. Ains se part mai
tenant de la cite et hercules et ses
compaignons le convoierent jus
ques au rivaige et illec lui conve
noit passer un petit bras de mer
pour aler en lisle ou li mouton
estoit. Il sarma de toutes ses ar
mes puis entra au batel sans nul
autre marinier et sen va droit a
lisle. Medea estoit montee sur une
tour. et quant le voit en mer ne
se pot tenir de plourer et dit tout
basset. beaux amis Jason en grant
erreur avez mon cueur mis. Car
Je vous ayme de si fine amour et
de si vraie que je nen puis estre
seure jusques a tant que je vous
voye revenir. Car je ne doubte
autre chose mais que vous nou
bliez riens de ce que je vous ay dit
et enseignez. Car jamais nauroie
joye en mon cueur. Pour quoy je
pri tous les dieux que ilz vous
soient amiables Comment Jason
conquist le toison sen retourna
en son pais.

En demantiers Jason atant
ale quil arriva a lisle et mai
tenant prent son escu et son glai
ne et sen ist hors du batel z chor

si les beuffs et le serpent et le
mouton q de fin or resplendissoit
et maintenant prist longuement
si en oint son corps et fait fia la
figure que medea lui bailla. puis
latacha sur son heaume apres
leut lestoupt trois foiz si comme
la pucelle li ot enseigne et main
tenant se tirant vers les beuffs q
tel feu et flambe gettoient que
maintenant fust son escu tout
ars se ne fust quil prist le gluz
et le leur espandi a la bouche
ne oncques puis flambe nen
yssi puis leur fist faire quatre
roies z quant il ot ce fait maintenant
ala le serpent requerre q si hi
deux estoit de feu sofvan que il
gettoit par mi la bouche et par
les narilles et de les batre et doubler
que il faisoit que mis home buiat

reduced

Folios 6v-7r, Jason seizing the golden fleece, having immobilized the sleepless dragon by drugging it and having killed Apsyrtus, brother of Medea, who watches from the battlements of a castle, set in a landscape with Jason's ship, the Argo, in full sail by the shore

iamais trouuer en cest pais se vous
amez voz vies. Quant antenor
et ses compaignons orent ce
ne demandez pas se ilz furent
espouentes Car bien saperceurent
que ilz vont querant folie et
par poy quilz ne sont trouues
si se remirent en leur nef et
retournerent en leur pais.

Comment Antenor reuint a
troye et redist son messaige

Et quant ilz furent par de
uant le roy venuz Ante
nor retraist son messaige en
la presence de touz les haulx
homes du pais si com il fu touz
premierement au roy releue et
apres a tous les autres et
les orgueilleuses menaces que
ilz auoient faictes au roy et a
li mesmes dont li roy ot moult
grant raison destre courrou
cie et si fu il moult. Et pour
ce le prist a retraire a ses filz
et a ses amis et dit beaux sei
gneurs veoir pouez comment
li gregois se maintiennent vers
nous Car apres le grant do
maige que ilz nous ont fait.
Voyez comment ilz nous pri
sent poy. or ne scay que ie vous
en die. fors tant que mieulx
ayme a mourir que souffrir tel
honte. Et ne soyons de riens

esmaiez de ce quilz orent contre
nous victoire. Car maintesfo[is]
auient que celui qui est vainc[u]
gaigne sur son ennemy et nous
auons forte ville et grant che[ua]
[lerie] Deuons estre desirant de
honte vengier toutesfoiz mett[ez]
laffaire sur vous que en faciez
vostre voulente non pas pour to[ut]
que la mort seroit comment qu
men deust auenir que nous ele[s]
sons tant de nre gent des plu[s]
hardis chiez que nous allisson[s]
celeement en leur pais. et ame[s]
que ilz sen apparceussent la ter[re]
fust toute confundue et les ho[mes]
mors et prinses les proyes et
qui tel orgueil peust abatre a
los et honneur nous tourneroi[t]
tourneroit et ce me semble le
re chose qui bien sen vouldroi[t]
pener a ce respondirent tous
bien leur plaisoit et de nul fu
contredit.

Comment li roy priant par[la]
a ses enffans

Adont appella li roy hecto[r]
son aisne filz et li dit. be[au]
filz tu es li chief de mes hom[mes]
serais sires et prince de cest[e]
euure Car tu en es bien di[gne]
apres appella tous ses autr[es]
filz et leur fist moult bea[u]
semblant Car preux beau

et hardiz sees droit et

leur dit vous serez de tres tous
sires et maistres apres vre sre
re hector. Mais gardez que vous
soyez telz com il affiert. Car
celui que je trouueray preux et
vaillant celui sera mes amis
et mes filz. Ore parestra latten
dance que je ay sre et quelle es
perance je puis avoir en ma
nourriture. Et je vous pourroye
assez dire et sermoner et se il
alast a ma voulente chun de
vous seroit tel que par lui tout
seul achieueroit sa besoigne. mais

tout demeure en vous de bien
faire. Car bien congnoissiez que
il vous couuient estre quant
vous estes tous princes et
maistres de si grant et de si
noble gent et de si grant euure
Or en facent li dieux mon plai
sir. La sage responce que hector
fist a son pere.

Hector que moult fu sages
respondi et dit. Sires voz
voulentez acompliray de tous
cuers voulentiers a mon pouoir
et de ce me trouuerez prest que
droit et raison me semble et
sachiez que je ne desir nulle
riens tant com de vengier nous
de celle gent q si por nous pri
sent. Car trop seroit laide chose
se de si grant tort ne fust ven
gence prise et de endroit de moy
ne desir tant nulle riens come
destre a celle esprouue. mais
moult nous couuient contre
garder sa chose en tel sens quel
le puisse prendre bonne fin.
Car ja soit li commancement
la plus grant partie de la cho
se ala fin apent quanque len
fait et celui commencement doit
estre moult haz dont la fin
est mauuaise. et pour ce vault
mieulx alaissier que emprendre
chose dont mal peust auenir

reduced

Folios 13v-14r, King Priam enthroned below a canopy, in conversation with his sons Hector, Paris, Deiphobus, Helenus and Troilus

11. Paris, Bibliothèque nationale de France, MS fr. 12602, late fifteenth century, on paper, incomplete, spaces left for miniatures never added.
12. London, British Library, Add. MS 9785, c. 1500, on paper, incomplete, no miniatures.

There is an earlier list of manuscripts by Marc-René Jung, *La légende de Troie*, 1996, pp. 442-43 and 455-84, incorporating copies also of a slightly different and revised text of "Prose 1," known as the *prose remaniée*, or later version. Including these too, the total number of manuscripts of different families of "Prose 1" now reaches eighteen or nineteen. The additions are:
13. Berlin, Staatsbibliothek, Cod. Hamilton 340, fifteenth century, incomplete, spaces left for 17 miniatures never added.
14. Cambridge, Trinity College, O.4.26, incomplete, 7 surviving miniatures (of 10).
15. Paris, Bibliothèque nationale de France, MS fr. 785, spaces left for 12 miniatures never added.
16. Paris, Bibliothèque nationale de France, MS fr. 1631, dated 1485, on paper, incomplete, no miniatures.
17. Paris, Bibliothèque nationale de France, MS fr. 24401, fifteenth century, incomplete, 23 miniatures with drawings and spaces left for others never added.
18. Saint Petersburg, Rossijskaja Nacional'naja Biblioteka, fr.F.v.XIV.12, early sixteenth century, 18 coloured drawings.
19. The manuscript listed by Jung on p. 442 as "Ophem, Bibl. du comte Hemricourt de Grunne (XVe s.)" on which no information appears to be published and may, in fact, be the present manuscript if it was acquired by that collection in 1938.

Every one of these, with the possible exception of the last, is in the inalienable possession of a European public collection. None is outside Europe. No other has come to the market since the present copy was sold in 1938. Each copy is slightly different and every one contributes to knowledge of the text; this manuscript has never been studied first-hand by any literary scholar.

The manuscript is missing 13 leaves. At least nine of the manuscripts above are also incomplete. The report of our copy by Constans (1912) cites its nineteenth-century owner as claiming that it had "environ 150 pages" (around 150 pages) and "une quarantaine" (approximately 40) fine miniatures. The former is only a guess (the complete manuscript had 122 folios) and, even if every missing leaf had a picture, which is unlikely, it can never have had more than 30, not 40. The numbers of leaves and miniatures now are exactly as they were when the manuscript was described by Quaritch in 1898.

Folio 17r, Paris (in golden armor) and other Trojan knights despoiling the temple of Venus and kidnapping Queen Helen, the most beautiful woman in the world

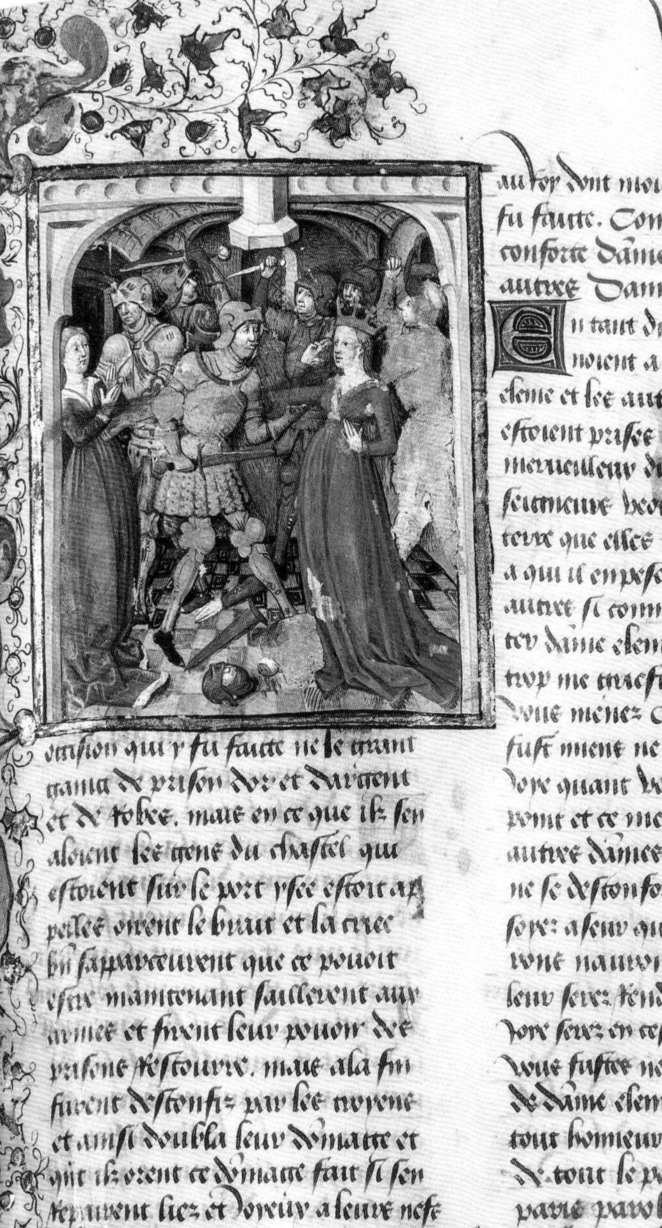

occision qui y fu faitte ne le grant
gaing de prison dor et dargent
et de robes. mais en ce que ilz sen
aloient les gens du chastel qui
estoient sur le port yssés estoit ap
pellees oirent le bruit et la crie
bien sapparceurent que ce pouoit
estre maintenant saillerent aux
armes et firent leur pouoir de
prisons rescourre. mais a la fin
furent desconfiz par les troyens
et ainsi doubla leur domaige et
quant ilz orent ce domaige fait si sen
retournerent liez et joyeux a leurs nefs
et landemain se partirent du port
et tant firent quilz arriverent a
Tanedon qui est a .v. lieues de
Troye si envoierent un messaige

au roy

au roy dont moult grant joye
fu faitte. Comment paris re
conforte dame eleine et les
autres dammes

En tant dis com ilz sejour
noient a tanedon. dame
eleine et les autres dames qui
estoient prises avec elle faisoient
merveilleux dueil de ce que leurs
seigneurs veoient pris et de leur
terre que elles laissoient paris
a qui il en pesoit sur touz les
autres si commenca a reconfor
ter dame eleine et dist. dame
trop me desplaist de la vie que
vous menez Car se tout li siecle
fust miens ne pourroye je avoir
joye quant vous fussiez en tel
point et ce mesme dit il aux
autres dames que pour dieu
ne se desconfortassent mie mais
soyez asseur que vous ne voz ba
rons nauront nul mal mais
leur serez rendues et a plus grant
joye serez en cest pais que la ou
vous fustes nees que pour lamour
de dame eleine vous fera len
tout honneur. Car elle sera dame
de tout le pais. Comment
paris parole a Eleine et
Eleine a lui

Sire ce respont dame eleine
moult me poise de ce que
avenu est mais puis que il est

reduced

Tant du siege qui dura si longue
ment et clami congnoist les grãs
destresses et le grant travail
que ilz mettent et leurs que si
est perilleuse si en ya de ceulx
a qui il plaist ce sont les jeu
nes bacheliers qui desirent
a faire d'armes mais tous les
plusieurs vouldroient avant
estre en leurs hostelz que da par
amour ne par force ne deuen
droient arriere. Comment li
roy dyomedes estoit destroit põ
la fille calcas de Troye

Mais qui que soit en joye et
en repos dyomedes a tout
le contraire que amour le tra

vaille en telle maniere que il ne
puet reposer Car celui ne puet
estre longuement en joye qui est
tourmentes par amour et de ce
dit aucun saiges que amour est
chose replaine dententive paour
et pour ce la loit il maintesfoiz
veoir et celle estoit a merveille sage
si congnoissoit bien au souspirer
et au regart que il estoit souspris
et pour ce li estoit anl tant plus
dure Car ce est naturel chose en
feme que se elle siet que vous la
mez a des vous sera plus orgueil
leuse et nulle foiz ne vous regarde
ra que ses yeulx ne soient plains
de fierte et de desdaing et moult
vendent chier le bien avant que
len lait et ce est moult contraire
chose que damer la ou len est hait
par semblant et grant merveille
est coment ce puet avenir et as
sez plus forte chose est quant un
home couvient prier celui ou
celle qui le despite. en telle manie
re se contient dyomedes com ce
lui qui souffrir ne sen puet Car
la avoit perdu le mangier et le
dormir et larmes et souspirs et
pleurs le font souvent veillier
et oublier toute ordre de raison et
soy mesmes et pour ce la prioit
autresfoiz moult engoissement
Car par fine force servient vul

reduced

The Meeting of Achilles and Hector, *Roman de Troie*, illuminated by the Master of Girart de Roussillon, c. 1450-1460 (Washington, D.C., National Gallery of Art, 1946.21.9), from missing fol. 43 of the present manuscript

In fact, one missing miniature from the present manuscript survives. It is B-13.519 (1946.21.9) among the Rosenwald cuttings in the National Gallery of Art in Washington, D.C. (Nordenfalk et al, 1975, pp. 185-87, no. 47), showing the meeting of Achilles and Hector. It belonged the collections of Edouard Warneck (1834-1924) and Arthur Sambon (1867-1947) before passing to Léonce Rosenberg by 1913. It is a fragment, cut close to the picture, not a whole leaf, which suggests the collecting taste of the earlier nineteenth century. The fragments of text on its verso correspond to parts of folios 75v and 76r of British Library Add. MS 9785 (no. 12 on the list above), which allows us to match it as part of the missing leaf 43 of the present manuscript. That fact was hitherto unknowable.

With the Washington cutting, the present manuscript had a cycle of at least eighteen miniatures, and probably more. This is almost unprecedented among manuscripts of the "Prose 1" text. Most are relatively humble copies. At least eight are on paper. Four have no pictures at all and six have spaces left for miniatures never completed. Only two have a larger repertoire of illustrations, no. 1, with twenty-five small thirteenth-century historiated initials, and no. 5, a paper manuscript with sixty-seven sketchy colored drawings. Judged at least from the standpoint of a luxury copy on parchment with fully colored and illuminated pictures, this is (even in its present condition) the finest and richest manuscript of the text extant.

Folio 50v, Diomedes visiting and falling in love with Cressida, daughter of the seer Calchas, set in a tent in a landscape with Diomedes' horse waiting behind

sauoir tiviolus que pour neant
sa tendroit a li des orez en auant.
Comt ilz se combatirent par vii
iours et apres requistrent triues

Or auint chose que li vi.
moys furent acomplies si
recommencerent leurs batailles
et se combatirent par vii. iours
que ilz ne departoient iusques
au soir si ot moult de gent occise
de chascune part mesmement de
haultes gens et de ceulx qui
naures estoient eschapperent
moult pou si pot decelle estre si
grant mortalite de gens de
mort naturel que dedans et de
hors en ot grant domage si leur
couuint demander triues si
manda Agamenon au roy priant
qui les donnast par xxx. iours
et il si fist si furent enterres li
mors et li malades tous rasoa
gies. li roy priant prenoit sou
uent conseil a ses filz et a ses
amis coment ilz se peussent
contregarder des choses qui leur
peussent nuire et de ce gramm
que valoir leur peust. ha las
quelle perte et quel douleur leur
auandra briefuement et que
pesant auenture ne star comt
de la puisse raconter ne vous
entendre que bien deussent
trestous a bon droit vouloir
la mort que tant furent puis
destruiz que iamais norent iop
or orres comment il auint en
ceste bataille que apres sera
que iamais telle perte ne tel do
mage nauendra en terre pour
la mort dun seul home et des
ores aparent les prophecies de
cassandra.

Comment la feme hettor song
la mort son baron

Les triues de xxx. iours fu
rent passees si sapareilla
chun pour estre landemain au
mortel tournoiemt q de male he
re comenca Et en celle mesme
nuit la feme hettor que andro
maca auoit nom moult bonne
dame et sage et auoit de son sei
gneur deux enffans moult peti
si auint q la nuit q les triues fu
rent finees elle vit par signes
et par auision q se hettor yssoit
a la bataille celui iour q il y de
uoit certainement morir par ce
ste demonstrance fot la dame la
destinee si ot de son seigneur
grant paour et ce ne fu pas
merueille. et pour ce parla a li
et li dit. Sire de vous vueil mo
strer por quelle chose ie suis entrée
en si grant paour q par pou li cue
ne me desine. li dieux qui ne veu
lent pas vre mort encore mont

reduced

Folios 51v-52r, Andromache, wife of Hector, pleads with her parents-in-law King Priam and Queen Hecuba and points to her infant son Astyanax who lies on the ground, set in a gothic parlor, detail

There are two or possibly three closely related hands in the miniatures here. We are immensely indebted to Professor Gregory Clark for his identification of the two principal hands as the illuminator known as the Master of Girart de Roussillon, who was almost certainly the documented illuminator to Philip the Good, Dreux Jean, also known as Dreux Bachoyer, who was appointed as court artist to the dukes of Burgundy in 1448 and remained in post until he was succeeded by Philippe de Mazerolles in 1467, the probable year of his death. Coincidentally, the attribution of the manuscript's missing miniature in Washington to Dreux Jean/Master of Girart de Roussillon was made independently by Hanno Wijsman on the TELMA database, "Luxury Bound," no. 3639.

The Master is named from an incomparable manuscript of the *Roman de Girart de Roussillon* made for Philip the Good in 1448, now in Vienna (ÖNB, cod. 2549), which is illuminated by the same artist as a roll chronicle of Jerusalem also made for the duke soon after 1455, also in Vienna (ÖNB, cod. 2533). Both are secular manuscripts of universal fame and astounding painterly quality. "The Girart Master's style is notable for its fusion of the traditions of Parisian illumination and south Netherlandish panel painting, as well as echoes of the work of both the Bedford Master and Rogier van der Weyden. Sophisticated landscapes, fine portraiture, an intense palette, and the distinctive juxtaposition of unblended colours are the hallmarks of the Girart Master's work"

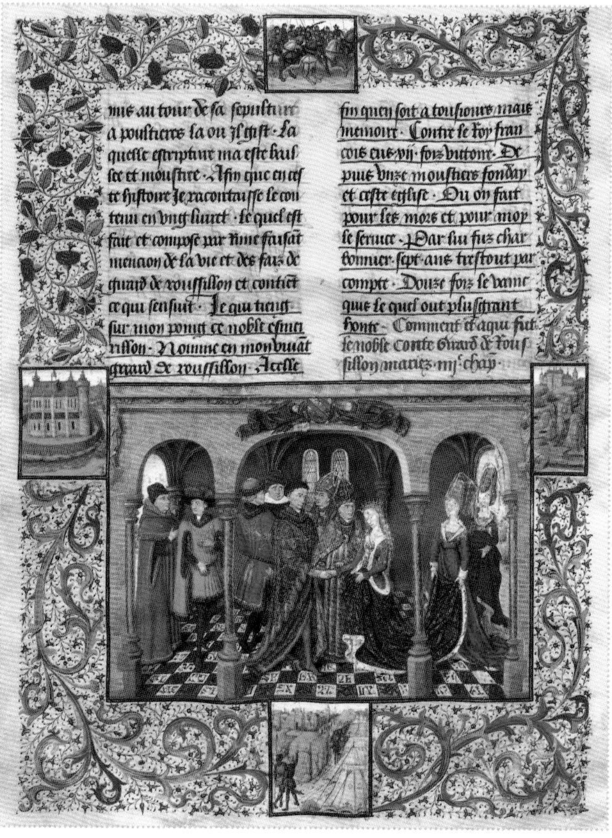

Marriage of Girart and Bertha, *Roman de Girart de Roussillon*, illuminated by the Master of Girart de Rousillon, after 1448 (Vienna, ÖNB, cod. 2549, fol. 9v)

Godfrey of Bouillon and Daimbert, *Chronicle of Jerusalem*, illuminated by the Master of Girart de Rousillon, after 1455 (Vienna, ÖNB, cod. 2533, fol. 2r, detail)

(McKendrick, *Illuminating the Renaissance*, 2003, p. 212). "In some cases he proves himself an excellent portrait painter, almost a rival of Rogier van der Weyden" (Dogaer, *Flemish Manuscript Painting*, 1987, p. 77). Anne van Buren called him simply the finest artist of his generation ("Dreux Jean and the *Grandes Heures* of Philip the Bold," 2002, p. 1403).

The case for identifying him with Dreux Jean hinges on the historical likelihood of the court painter from 1448 being the principal artist of two of the duke's greatest manuscripts from that period and from two miniatures added in the *Grandes Heures* of Philip the Bold (Cambridge, Fitzwilliam Museum, MS 3-1954, fols. 238v and 256r), a manuscript documented as updated in 1451 by several artists, including Dreux Jean. The identification is accepted as overwhelmingly probable but just short of proven. Dreux Jean was born in Paris and was working in Bruges before his appointment as illuminator to Philip the Good in 1448. In 1449 he was the duke's *valet de chambre*, and he was salaried as court illuminator to the prince of Valois until 1454. In 1464, Charles the Bold renewed his contract as ducal illuminator and *valet de chambre*.

Professor Clark emphasizes to us the identity of the principal artist here with that of the finest paintings of the *Roussillon* itself and the Jerusalem chronicle. This is important, for there is a widening circle of manuscripts in related style but not necessarily all by the same painter. The probability is that the Master of Girart de Roussillon directed an intimate workshop. The absolute core work by his own hand is perhaps no more than three or four manuscripts, in Vienna and Brussels. The only manuscript of the larger group outside continental Europe is Los Angeles, J. Paul Getty Museum, MS Ludwig XI.8, almost certainly no closer than very loosely in the style of the workshop. The addition of a newly attributed manuscript to the elusive and incomparable Master himself is a major event in the scholarship of southern Netherlandish art.

The Master of Girart de Roussillon executed the miniatures here on folios 1r, 4v, 14r, 17r, 18v, 50v, 52r, 63v and 107r. These are superbly colored paintings showing rich costumes and intimacy of human interaction, set in luminous landscapes. The same artist probably painted the miniatures on folios 7r, 69v, 119r and 120v. A recognizably different artist but working within the Master's style produced the miniatures on folios 60r, 61v, 84v and 106r. These enchanting scenes are everything that popular imagination associates with the romance of the Middle Ages, including kings and princes, damsels and queens, ships, castles and chivalry. The manuscript is rich in details of costume and courtly regalia, as ancient myth is reset into the landscape of the Netherlands. The image of Achilles and Ajax playing chess, reproduced in all three sale catalogues of 1931-37, is one of the finest medieval depictions of the game. When this manuscript was first offered for auction in 1931, the catalogue broke into capitals, "FINELY ILLUSTRATED LITERARY MANUSCRIPTS OF THE BURGUNDIAN SCHOOL ARE EXCEPTIONALLY RARE" and, if that was true then, they are incomparably rarer on the market now nearly 90 years later. This is probably the finest manuscript of Trojan romance ever likely to be sold again.

Folio 60r, the funeral of Hector, with the Trojan kings and noblemen and women gathering in sorrow around his tomb

...chierte si grant en lost que
...pain y valoit un besant et la
...r dun beuff .v. marc si prirent
...nseil de liopev a pourchacier
...ande et ne stay se par mal...
...e fu fait q ilz y tramirent
...amenon q onques de rient
...sen de sautina car de grant
...e estoit si ne vouloit mie que
...un destourbier en sourdist dot
...pouoir fust plus foible si es
...grant compaignie de chevaliers

...servans et alerent par tout
...ut et refreschi lost de tout
...si q moult fu bien faicte la
...oisie et moult pleut a ceulx

de lost. Endementiers palame
des q moult estoit de grant pouv
pens fist rapareillier toute
la navie et ratirer tous leurs
affaires et ce mesmes firent
ceulx de la cite car ilz rapareil
lerent leurs murs et leurs tonelles
et refirent leurs engins et
toutes leurs deffaultes pfirent
par le tirant loisir que ilz orent

Coment lanniversaire dector fu fait
au chief de lan que il fu mort

Endementiers q ilz faisoient
ce et q les trives duroient
si fu acompli li an q hector avoit
este mort si ne fu onques fait

reduced

ronne estoit devant eulx et
la pucelle nentint autre plait
et nen fist semblant que lee
li soit ne que de riens li en
pesast.

Comment la royne Ecuba respondi au messaige Achilles

Quant la royne vit le mes
saige revenu si li dit tou
te la response au roy priant et
pour ce que la chose estoit mer
...

damour
de riens
dolant et
seure faut
tes choses

les a aucu
et ce est li
seure en
les qui
telle mani
Achilles

PHYSICAL DESCRIPTION

reduced

The Romance of Troy, binding

3 paper flyleaves + 109 folios on parchment + 3 paper flyleaves, lacking 13 leaves (one blank), modern pencil foliation 1-122 in upper outer rectos takes account of missing leaves (although they were already missing before the book was foliated), collation: i8, ii7 [of 8, lacking i = '9'], iii-iv8, v7 [of 8, lacking v = '37'], vi6 [of 8, lacking iii and v = '43' and '46'], vii-ix8, x6 [of 8, lacking iv-v = '76'-'77'], xi6 [of 8, lacking ii and vi = '82' and '86'], xii6 [of 8, lacking i and vi = '89' and '94'], xiii7 [of 8, lacking viii = '104', with missing text copied into the lower margin of fol. 103v], xiv7 [of 8, lacking vii = '118'], xv9 [of 10, lacking x, blank at end], with horizontal catchwords; ruled in pale red ink, justification 212 x 150 mm., two columns of 34 lines, written in dark brown ink in a professional slightly sloping *lettre bâtarde*, some first and last lines (especially at ends of quires) with elaborate decorative cadels extending far into upper and lower margins, headings in bright red; two-line initials throughout in burnished gold on red and blue grounds with white tracery and marginal sprays of pairs of gold leaves within black penwork, some illuminated line-fillers at ends of paragraphs; seventeen large miniatures with richly illuminated borders of colored acanthus leaves and burnished gold bezants and bryony leaves within brown penwork, one miniature 2 columns wide (folio 60r), seven miniatures spreading into the adjacent column and sometimes into the margins as well, four other column-width miniatures spreading into one or more margins; some wear, some miniatures a bit rubbed with minor loss of pigment and spots of smudging, occasionally extremities of wide illuminated borders slightly cropped, some stains and creasing and signs of thumbing, first outer margin slightly frayed, generally in sound and often excellent state for a much-used secular text; bound in old (seemingly even contemporary) reversed skin over pasteboards sewn on 4 thongs, paper pastedowns, rebacked with old spine laid on, old MS spine title "GUER/RE DE TROIE", in an English full red morocco fitted case gilt. Dimensions 310 x 230 mm.

Folio 4v, Medea the sorceress, daughter of King Aeëtes, seated on a bench in a gothic room in conversation with Jason, with whom she falls in love, attended by an armed knight, detail

de touz noz ennemis com celui q
moult estoit espris de samour et
moult tient preux men a fait seu
re or scay pour voir que il ne les
puet faire partir pourquoy il le
nous a fait chier comparer q
soubz ceste paix et soubz ceste
fiance si a ton frere oste pour
quoy je le vueil mander que il

TEXT

The manuscript opens on folio 1r, "*Ci commence li prologue de la vraie hystoire de Troye*, Li anciens sages que de philosophie erent ...." The second leaf, which would be the clue to eventual identification in the Burgundian or other courtly inventories, begins "Grece est moult grant." The text ends on folio 121v, "... estre tenue et comme il fu etc. Explicit la vraie histoire de Troye."

ILLUMINATION

The miniatures are:

1. Folio 1r, Philosophers instructing a king, perhaps King Laomedon, who is seated below a canopy in a gothic throne room, 16 lines, 100 x 75 mm.; two-sided floral border including a putto with a trumpet and a lion-footed grotesque in the foliage with pendulous breasts and a hat lined with ermine.

2. Folio 4v, Medea the sorceress, daughter of King Aeëtes, seated on a bench in a gothic room in conversation with Jason, with whom she falls in love, attended by an armed knight, 14 lines, 89 x 72 mm.; two-sided floral border including apes attacking each other with spear and bow and arrow and an angel playing a lute.

3. Folio 7r, Jason seizing the golden fleece, having immobilized the sleepless dragon by drugging it and having killed Apsyrtus, brother of Medea, who watches from the battlements of a castle, set in a landscape with Jason's ship, the Argo, in full sail by the shore, 13 lines, 82 x 73 mm.; two-sided floral border.

4. Folio 14r, King Priam enthroned below a canopy, in conversation with his sons Hector, Paris, Deiphobus, Helenus and Troilus, 19 lines, 118 x 81 mm.; two-sided floral border including an archer shooting an ape and a Wildman grasping foliage.

5. Folio 17r, Paris (in golden armor) and other Trojan knights despoiling the temple of Venus and kidnapping Queen Helen, the most beautiful woman in the world, 16 lines, 100 x 85 mm.; floral border extending into two margins.

6. Folio 18v, Menelaus, jilted husband of Helen, in conversation with his brother Agamemnon, meeting on horseback in a landscape attended by other Greek noblemen, 15 lines, 97 x 76 mm.; floral border extending into two margins.

7. Folio 50v, Diomedes visiting and falling in love with Cressida, daughter of the seer Calchas, set in a tent in a landscape with Diomedes' horse waiting behind, 17 lines, 108 x 81 mm.; floral border extending into two margins.

8. Folio 52r, Andromache, wife of Hector, pleads with her parents-in-law King Priam and Queen Hecuba and points to her infant son Astyanax who lies on the ground, set in a gothic parlor, 14 lines, 92 x 75 mm.; marginal floral border.

9. Folio 60r, The funeral of Hector, with the Trojan kings and noblemen and women gathering in sorrow around his tomb, 18 lines, two-column, 120 x 151 mm.; marginal floral border.

Folio 84v, a messenger receiving orders from Queen Hecuba who lies on her bed planning vengeance for the deaths of her sons, set in a castle with women listening at the door, detail

deux filz hector

Dautre part resist tant Aga
menon que Cassandra luy
fu ottroyee Car si come nous trou
uons il lauoit amee par amour
merueilleusement et ainsi fu
rent des autres dames et pucel
les donnees aux autres prin
cessement vn iour vint antenor
au consile et pria trestous que
elenus li filz le roy priant et an
dromata fussent quites que
celle guerre auoient deffendue
assez deuant que elle comencast
et coment elenus auoit moult
bn dit a son pere priant et a tous
les autres quelle en seroit la
fin de ceste guerre et apres auo
ient fait rendre le corps Achil
les q ilz vouloient trainer et pe
dre vilainemnt Sur ce fu respon
du assez diuersemt mais a la
fin saccorderent que ilz fussent
quites et quant elenus fu deliu
re li et son auoir si pria pour sa
mere la royne Ecuba q rendue
li fust et la retint pirrus auec
soy apres fist quiter les deux
filz hettor q li grieux auoient
iuges a mort et apres iniftres
sur li del aler ou du demourer
a sa voulente. Comment li
auoir fu departi

Dautre auoir partirent
puis tout par acort toutesfoiz
les plus riches choses furent
donees aux plus prisies selon ce
q ilz y auoient plus fait Apres
parlerent de leur alee mais si
horrible estoit la mer que elle
ne monstroit q iamais nulz
home y deust entrer dedans et
ce dura plus de vn mois si distret
a calcas q il enqueist q ce estoit
et cil ala et fist ses sors et dist
que iamais les enfernalz furies
ne laisseroient la mer en paix
se ilz neussent leur droiture et
vengeance de larme Achilles.

Comment polixenam fu
trouuee et iugee a mort

Adonc se pensa pirrus ou estoit
celle par qui il auoit este
mort ou se elle viuoit encore
assez en demanda mais chun
disoit que il ne la sauoit mie
et que puis que la cite fu pri
se ny ot nul qui la veist. Si ala
tant la parole que Antenor en
fu blasmes Si lenquerroit Aga
menon et en parla a eneas et
il dist que il ne la sauoit mie
et se il la sceust ne la celeroit
pas mais Antenor li cruel
la quist tant que il la trou
ua vn iour en vne chambre
dune vieille tournelle ou
eneas lauoit amuchee si

reduced

Folio 105v-106r, the Greeks arresting Polyxena, who was being held as hostage, and debating whether she should be sacrificed at the end of the Trojan War, set in a castle hall

10. Folio 61v, Achilles in his tent listening to and falling in love with Polyxena, daughter of King Priam, who kneels before him, set in a landscape of castles, 16 lines, 106 x 103 mm., marginal floral border.

11. Folio 63v, The legate of Achilles negotiating with Queen Hecuba in her bedroom, while a maid sits on the floor playing with a dog, 16 lines, 103 x 98 mm.; marginal floral border.

12. Folio 69v, Achilles and Ajax playing chess in a tent, as Trojan knights in gold and silver armor remonstrate at their idleness, 16 lines, 103 x 92 mm.; marginal floral border.

13. Folio 84v, A messenger receiving orders from Queen Hecuba who lies on her bed planning vengeance for the deaths of her sons, set in a castle with women listening at the door, 21 lines with extension into two margins, 166 x 126 mm.; floral border including grapes extending into three margins.

14. Folio 106r, The Greeks arresting Polyxena, who was being held as hostage, and debating whether she should be sacrificed at the end of the Trojan War, set in a castle hall, 21 lines, 130 x 123 mm.; floral border extending into two margins.

15. Folio 107r, Queen Hecuba being stoned beside the golden tomb of Achilles, attended by a large number of noblemen and women, 20 lines, 131 x 133 mm.; floral border extending into three margins.

16. Folio 119r, Landomata, son of Hector, returning to Troy and ordering the execution of Calchas, who is hanged from a tree, 20 lines with marginal extension, 187 x 143 mm.; floral border in lower margin.

17. Folio 120v, Landomata imprisoning the king of Armenia in a white tower and taking the throne for himself, 20 lines, 130 x 119 mm.; floral border extending into two margins.

PROVENANCE

1. Doubtless written for a member of the court of the dukes of Burgundy, possibly Charles the Bold himself, for whom reputed descent from the Trojans was paramount. The arms hanging on the tent in the miniature on folio 61v, quarterly *or* and *azure*, were borne by the family of Tournemine of Brittany and it has been suggested that the manuscript was illuminated for Gilles de Tournemine (d. 1474), celebrated soldier and patron of British Library, Harley MS 5781. However, the arms are not shown in a position of proprietorship and the manuscript is not Breton. There was a branch of the family of Tournemine in Lille, principally mercers, which is at least geographically more plausible.

Léopold Constans proposed instead that the manuscript may have belonged to the library of the Château de Montbeton, near Montaubon, close to where it was first recorded in the nineteenth century: the inventory of its very small library in 1495 included a "Histoire de Troie." The château was then owned by the family of St-Étienne.

2. There are nineteenth-century inscriptions on the flyleaf and pastedown, "Capus" and "Capus au Théron, comune de Cestayrols," probably Jean-Antoine-Raymond-Euzèbe-Prosper-Grégoire Capus; he was born 1829 and was still head of the family when A. B.

Folio 119r, Landomata, son of Hector, returning to Troy and ordering the execution of Calchas

celui respondi quil ne vouloit mie
que il laissast son pais Anchili
des li donna grant partie de ses
meilleurs chiez et a toute grant
gens sen mistrent en mer tant
que ilz arriverent en turquie
la mesmes ou troye avoit este
et trouua que vn neveu Ante
nor que druas avoit nom avoit
forteresses fermees pres de troye
et traveilloit les gens du pais
a son pouoir et les tenoit en grant
servaige ceulx qui demouroient y
estoient et maint autres peuple
avoient de tous leurs
voisins environ ne p
tro ne sen savoient Car
dure chose est de laiss
le pais ou len est nez et
nourris et ses ancesseurs
comment que len y soit a mes
chief. Comment landomatha
li filz hector retorna a troye

Quant landomatha fu
arrivez a troye et
cilz du pais sorent sa ve
nue si se traistrent mai
tenant entour li tous et se
plaignent du grant mal
quilz souffroient et nes
mement du lait servaige
ou druas le neveu ante
nor les tenoit quant ce
entendi landomatha si li

li vindrent les lermes aux yeulx
Car si tost par nature en ot grant pitie
et pource fist maintenant armer sa
gent pour aler sur druas et cil
fu si outrecuidiez quil li vint aler
contre ou tout grant gent la bataille
se assembla moult grant mais
ala fin fu druas desconfit et pris
et morte la plus grant partie
de sa gent et il mesmes fu pris si
le fist landomatha escorchier tout
vif et puis pendre a une grosse
chaine de fer et dit que ce li fist
il faire en vengence de sa trai

reduced

Bardou published his *Famille Capus, du Théron-sur-Cestayrols (Tarn)*, Albi, 1898. Théron was then a village of only 24 houses, where the Capus family had lived since at least the time of Pierre Capus de Théron around 1600. It is approximately 14 km. north-west of Albi in southern France. In 1894 the Capus family unsuccessfully offered the manuscript for sale to the Bibliothèque nationale.

3. Bernard Quaritch, London, *Manuscripts, Bibles and Liturgies*, cat. 176, January 1898, no. 22, at the then considerable price of £440.

4. John Thomas Adams (c.1849-1931), manufacturer of polishes, Sheffield; his sale, Sotheby's, 7 December 1931, lot 59, with folding plate.

5. William Harrison Woodward (1856-1941), Professor of Education, University of Liverpool; his sale, Sotheby's, 14 June 1937, lot 508, with color plate; bought by the London bookseller, G. Michelmore; his *Rare and Choice Books ... including the Tournemaine Illuminated Ms. of the Roman de Troie*, cat. 27 (1938), no. 148, and color frontispiece.

6. Private collection, small gilt book label of a rising bird, MS 6.

PUBLISHED REFERENCES

Although none of the writers had seen it or knew its location, the present manuscript is cited in:

L. CONSTANS, *Le Roman de Troie par Benoît de Sainte-Maure, publié d'après tous les manuscrits connus*, VI, Paris, 1912, pp. 271-72.

B. WOLEDGE, *Bibliographie des Romans et Nouvelles en prose française antérieurs à 1500*, Publications Romanes et Françaises XLVII, Geneva and Lille, 1954, p. 126.

C. NORDENFALK, WITH C. FERGUSON, D. S. STEVENS SCHAFF AND G. VIKAN, *Medieval and Renaissance Miniatures from the National Gallery of Art*, Washington, 1975, pp. 186-87.

M.-R. JUNG, *La légende de Troie en France ay moyen âge, Analyse des versions françaises et bibliographie raisonnée des manuscrits*, Romanica Helvetica 114, Basel and Tübingen, 1996, pp. 442 and 466.

A. M. GAUTHIER, "Édition et étude critique du 'cycle des Retours' du *Roman de Troie* de Benoît de Saint-Maure," PhD diss., University of Montréal, 1997, p. 339.

M. GIL, "Le cycle d'illustration du *Roman de Troie* en prose be Benoît de Sainte-Maure dans le milieu bourguignon," in J.-C. Herbin, ed., *Richesses médiévales du Nord et du Hainaut*, Valenciennes, 2002, pp. 155-83, at pp. 165-66.

F. VIELLIARD, "*Du Roman de Troie* à la 'vraie estoire de Troie' (*Prose 1*, version commune): le choix de l'Histoire," in L. Harf-Lancner et al., eds., *Conter de Troie et d'Alexandre, Pour Emmanuèle Baumgartner*, Paris, 2006, pp. 177-93, at p. 179, n. 11.

D. E. BOOTON, *Manuscripts, Market and the Transition to Print in Late Medieval Brittany*, Farnham and Burlington, 2010, p. 283.

Folio 120v, Landomata imprisoning the king of Armenia in a white tower and taking the throne for himself, detail

...ut iwm
...ect
...e en
...y et

Li roi ligos darmenie fist il mett
en vne fierx pson = ne li faisoit
doner boire ne meng: tat q vn do li fistil

FURTHER LITERATURE

For the general background on the "Prose 1" text of the romance of Troy, and on the work of the Master of Girart de Roussillon, in addition to items already cited, see also:

BOSSUAT, R. *Manuel bibliographique de la littérature française du Moyen Âge*, Paris, 1955, p. 88, nos. 6795-96.

CASPAR, G., AND F. LYNA, *Philippe le Bon et ses beaux livres*, Brussels, 1944.

CROIZY-NAQUET, C. "*Le Roman de Troie* en prose et le monde païen antique," *Études médiévales* 4 (2002): 197-205.

DOUTREPONT, G. *La littérature française à la cour des ducs de Bourgogne*, Paris, 1909.

DURAND, C. "L'illustration du *Roman de Troie* et de ses dérivés dans les manuscrits français," PhD diss., École des hautes études en sciences sociales, Paris, 2003.

ROCHEBOUET, A. AND A. SALAMON, "Les échecs et la cite de Troie," *La règle du jeu, Questes* 18 (2010): 30-43 (available online).

TANNIOU, F. "'*Raconter la vraie estoire de Troie*,' Histoire et édification dans le *Roman de Troie* en prose," PhD diss., Université de Paris X-Nanterre, 2009.

And for the artist:

DOGAER, G. *Flemish Manuscript Painting in the 15th and 16th Centuries*, Amsterdam, 1987, pp. 77-83.

CLARK, G. "Le Maître du Girart de Roussillon (Dreux Jeahan)," in B. Bousmanne and T. Delcourt, eds., *Miniatures flamandes, 1404-1482*, Paris and Brussels, 2011, especially pp. 188-91.

KREN, T., AND S. McKENDRICK, Eds., *Illuminating the Renaissance, The Triumph of Flemish Manuscript Painting in Europe*, Los Angeles, 2003, pp. 212-16.

PÄCHT, O., U. JENNI AND D. G. THOSS, *Flämische Schule*, I, Die Illuminierten Handschriften und Inkunabeln der Österreichischen Nationalbibliothek 6, Vienna, 1983, esp. pp. 50-51.

VAN BUREN, A. "Dreux Jean and the *Grandes Heures* of Philip the Bold," in B. Cardon, J. Van der Stock and D. Vanwijnsberghe, eds., '*Als ich can', Liber Amicorum in Memory of Professor Dr. Maurits Smeyers*, Corpus of Illuminated Manuscripts from the Low Countries 9, Louvain, 2002, pp. 1377-1414.

WIJSMAN, H. *Luxury Bound: Illustrated Manuscript Production and Noble and Princely Book Ownership in the Burgundian Netherlands (1400-1550)*, Turnhout, 2010 (and associated corpus compiled for the online database www.cn-telma.fr//luxury-bound).

PROJECT STAFF :

COPY EDITOR

MATTHEW WESTERBY

DESIGN

VIRGINIE ENL'ART

PHOTOGRAPHY

RACHEL HANEL (1)

JACQUES TORREGANO (2-4)

PROJECT MANAGER

GAIA GRIZZI

PRINTED IN ITALY

VERONA, e-graphic

DISTRIBUTION

PAUL HOLBERTON PUBLISHING

89 BOROUGH HIGH STREET, LONDON, SE1 1NL

WWW.PAUL-HOLBERTON.NET

FOR SANDRA HINDMAN, *LES ENLUMINURES*

PARIS, CHICAGO, AND NEW YORK

Les Enluminures

PARIS • CHICAGO • NEW YORK